Becoming a Servant *After* God's Own Heart

EDDIE HEDGES

ISBN 979-8-88832-464-6 (paperback)
ISBN 979-8-88832-465-3 (digital)

Christian Faith Publishing
832 Park Avenue
Meadville, PA 16335
www.christianfaithpublishing.com

Unless otherwise indicated, Scripture quotations are from the King James Version of the Bible.

Scripture taken from the HOLY BIBLE, NEW INTERNATIONAL VERSION. Copyright 1973, 1978, 1984 by International Bible Society. Used by permission Zondervan Publishing House. All rights reserved.

The "NIV" and "New International Version" trademarks are registered in the United State Patent and Trademark Office by International Bible society. Use of either trademark requires the permission of International Bible Society.

Scripture taken from the NEW AMERICAN STANDARD BIBLE, Copyright 1960, 1962,1963, 1968, 1971, 1972, 1973, 1975, 1977, 1995 by The Lockman Foundation. Used by permission.

Printed in the United States of America

CONTENTS

ABOUT THE COVER

As we start this journey together about becoming a servant after God's own heart, I wanted the cover of this book to be a message as well. I tried to put symbolism of God and salvation through Jesus into it. I hope you grasp the message I am trying to convey in the cover of this Bible study.

There are two hearts, representing our pursuit of becoming the servant God wants us to be. The heart on the right side of the cover symbolizes God's heart. It is deep red in color, representing royalty or the sovereignty of God. There is a glow behind this heart showing God's holiness and righteousness, and that He is to be reverenced.

Between the two hearts is the cross, which symbolizes Jesus and His death and resurrection to redeem us from the penalty of our sins. On the cross are two verses of scripture, both of which reveal Jesus as the only way to eternal life in heaven. The cross represents Jesus who connects the two hearts together.

The second heart represents the redeemed child of God and those of us who are pursuing a heart after God's own heart. It is white in color, symbolizing that our sins have been forgiven, and they are white as snow, as stated in the Bible.

At the top of the cross is a dove, which represents the Holy Spirit. The Holy Spirit is our comforter, counselor, guide, and teacher. It is God's Spirit living in us.

At the foot of the cross, or the foundation, are the Holy Bible and hands folded in prayer. These are both the foundation of our spiritual growth and drawing near to God. There are also additional scriptures that explain that Jesus is Lord and Savior.

The letters in the title of the book are in deep red, representing the blood of Jesus that he shed to redeem us from our sins. Jesus is the risen Lord and Savior.

The background color is blue, like the sky, and is symbolic of God's love. As the sky covers the whole earth, God's love covers the entire world and all of mankind—God is love.

Throughout this study, we will discuss four incredible gifts from God—Jesus, the Holy Spirit, the Holy Bible, and prayer. These are covered in detail in Session 4. All four of the gifts are highlighted on the cover.

On a personal note, I want to give special thanks to my beautiful wife, Elaine. She has been a constant encourager and has shared her thoughts and ideas into this study, as well as spending numerous hours editing its content. She has worked diligently with me on the cover. All of her assistance has been invaluable. *Proverbs 31:12 (NIV)* shows all about her input and guidance: "She brings him good, and not harm, all the days of her life." Truly, she is my most valuable asset.

SESSION 1

Introduction

Disclosures: I don't claim to be a biblical scholar, so please don't take everything I say as biblical truth. You should search the Bible yourself for biblical truth and pray that the Holy Spirit will lead, guide, and teach you what is and is not the truth from God.

Anytime there is a human element involved in biblical study, there can be error. Accordingly, some of what I say are only my thoughts and interpretation of the Scriptures. Let the Holy Spirit guide you throughout this study.

Also, many things I bring out may be repeated again throughout this study. What applies in one area will apply in other areas as well.

Another introductory comment is that I will ask questions throughout our study. Sometimes, the questions are to promote discussion within a group setting. In this case, I will provide my own personal comments to add to the discussion. Other times, the questions are to encourage you to give thought to what we are studying at that time and determine how it may apply to the current topic we are focusing on during that portion of our study.

Since this is a Bible study, I encourage you to read each passage of scripture out of your own Bible as we discuss them. I also suggest that you underline, mark, or highlight those verses that are meaningful to you.

So let's start off with a question: *What do you want to gain from this study of becoming a servant after God's own heart?*
Here are my goals for this study:

- Spiritual growth. This will be a life-long pursuit to grow stronger spiritually every day, week, month, and year throughout your entire life. This is vital to becoming a servant after God's own heart.
- Gain insight in how to make a difference in not only your life but also in the lives of others—family, friends, relationships, work environment, and church. This is actually an offshoot of spiritual growth.
- Personal observation. It is my belief that in everything you are involved in, it should be better because you are a part of it. Did you make it better? Especially, did you make a godly and spiritual difference?

First, look at "making a difference in the lives of others." Let's start with these quotes from leadership expert John Maxwell: "You don't eat the fruit or harvest the crop the day you plant the seed." In some cases, you may not even see the harvest of the seeds you plant. "You cannot harvest *where* you have not planted. You cannot harvest *what* you have not planted." I would add, "You cannot harvest *if* you have not planted." And lastly, "Your candle loses nothing when it lights another." Often, when you light someone else's candle, they in turn will light the candles in the lives of others. And it continues to compound or multiply.

With that thought in mind, what is the definition of compounding? Trust me, there is a point I want to make in asking this question.

Let me give you an illustration of compounding. Suppose someone came to you and offered to hire you to work for them for thirty months. They offered you a choice of compensation.

First, they offered to pay you $500,000 at the end of this thirty-month period. Nice salary, and I think that is something on which we all can agree. Or they offered to pay you monthly with your first month's compensation being one cent. The next month, your salary would double to two cents, then double the next month to four cents, with each month's salary doubling monthly during the thirty-month period. Which method of compensation would you choose?

If you chose the second compensation package, your salary for the thirtieth month would be $5,368,709.12.

I realize this is not realistic; however, I am trying to make a point of how important the concept of compounding can be in many areas of your life, as well as your personal financial position.

Many people do not understand the concept of compounding. It is a term mostly used in financial circles. A majority of economists believe the power of compounding is the most powerful force in building wealth.

Basically, compounding is taking the earnings from an investment and reinvesting the earnings, along with the principal investment, so you can make even more money. In other words, it is earnings on earnings. A simple illustration would be if you invested $1,000 at 10 percent for one year; you would earn $100. If you then added the $100 earnings to the original principal of $1,000, the new principal balance would be $1,100. That amount invested at 10 percent for one year would then earn $110. Continuing the process, you would now have $1,210 to invest; whereas if you spent the earnings each year, you would have only the original $1,000 to invest. Money invested at 10 percent per annum and compounded annually will actually double itself in approximately 7.5 years. So using the illustration above, you would have approximately $2,000 at the end of 7.5 years.

Something that is important to remember in compounding is that it starts very slowly, but over time, it will explode. If you will analyze my example of working for thirty months, you will see what I am saying. Do the math for yourself, and you will see the impact.

But how do you unleash the power of compounding in your life? I think it is important to emphasize that compounding can be used in many areas of your life and for many beneficial and useful purposes.

So *in the context of this study, how can compounding apply?* You take what you learn and teach it to others and apply it in your life as a witness and a testimony. Maybe you teach a class over this study or teach your children and grandchildren. Perhaps you mentor someone, teach a group, or share a portion of the study—the spiritual, life-application issues. God does not use each of us in the same way, but He will use you if you will let Him.

Think of the impact of becoming a servant after God's own heart could have on building the kingdom of God.

Psalm 78:1–7 (NIV) states:

> O my people, hear my teaching, listen to the words of my mouth. I will open my mouth, in parables, I will utter hidden things, things from of old—what we have heard and known, what our fathers have told us. We will not hide them from their children; we will tell the next generation the praiseworthy deeds of the LORD, his power, and the wonders he had done. He decreed statutes for Jacob and established the law in Israel, which he commanded our forefathers to teach their children, so the next generation would know them, even the children yet to be born, and they in turn would tell their children. Then they would put their trust in God and would not forget his deeds but would keep his commands.

Do you see the principle of compounding in this passage? Some additional passages supporting this come from *Psalm 89:1–2 and John 15:1–5, 8.* Notice the progression, multiplication, or compounding stated in these verses.

As each generation passes away, a new generation must be born, raised up, and taught to place their faith and trust in Jesus and God, our Creator.

From the passage in Psalm 78, the great things God has done are not just what is from the Bible. They are also the great things He has done in our lives individually and as a church. They are to be shared with others, even with generations yet to come.

Maybe, just maybe, the things you gain in your personal, spiritual growth are taught to others and will live on even after you have gone to be with the Lord in heaven. This is something that will be discussed throughout this study—you can take it with you by leaving it behind. Keep this thought in mind as we go through this study.

To expand this part of making a difference in the lives of others, what is your definition of success? My definition of success is becoming the person that God wants you to be and being a good steward with the time, talents, gifts, and opportunities He has given you.

What is the definition of steward or stewardship? What is the definition of trustee? A steward is a person in charge of another's business or assets. A trustee is a person who holds and manages property for another. *How does being a steward and/or a trustee apply to this study?* We are God's stewards and trustees to manage and oversee all He has entrusted to us.

Look at the following:

> Moreover, it is required in stewards, that a man be found faithful. (*1 Corinthians 4:2 KJV*)

> Guard, through the Holy Spirit who dwells in us, the treasure which has been entrusted to you. (*2 Timothy 1:14 NASB*)

> Timothy, guard what has been entrusted to your care. (*1 Timothy 6:20 NIV*)

Replace Timothy with your name. We are to guard and protect what has been entrusted to our care.

Matthew 25:21 (KJV) says, "His lord said unto him, Well done, thou good and faithful servant; thou hast been faithful over a few things, I will make thee ruler over many things. Enter thou into the joy of thy lord."

From this verse, do you see two promises from God when we are good stewards?

- He will make you ruler over many things.
- We will enter into the joy of the Lord.
- As we develop and mature in our stewardship, God is able to entrust us with more of His resources. Good stewardship in a little means being entrusted with more. God rewards faithfulness with new opportunities and responsibilities because He knows we will handle what He entrusts to us. *Think about this—why would God entrust you with more when you have not been faithful with what He has already entrusted to you?* We are God's stewards and trustees to grow and expand His kingdom.

What are some things we should be a faithful steward or trustee over?

- Money (*Matthew 25:14–30*)
- Family (*Deuteronomy 6:4–9*)
- Work (*Colossians 3:23–24*)
- Time (*Ephesians 5:15–16*)
- Faith (*Luke 12:42–48*)
- Our physical bodies (*1 Corinthians 3:16 and 1 Corinthians 6:19–20*)
- Resources (*Genesis 1:26*)
- Relationships (*Luke 16:10–12*). This could cover many areas of life, including relationships. *Proverbs 25:19 (NIV)* says, "Like a bad tooth or a lame foot is reliance on the unfaithful in times of trouble." Are you trustworthy and reliable? Comment: If you cannot trust someone *all* the time, then you cannot trust them *any* of the time because you never know when the time will be that you should not trust them.

Look now at *Proverbs 18:16 (NIV):* "A gift opens the way for the giver, and ushers him into the presence of the great." *What do you think this verse means?* In the context of this study, the gift would be the talents, gifts, and opportunities God has given you, and when you are faithful and obedient to use your talents, gifts, and opportunities, you are ushered into the presence of the great; or God will use you to do great things, even beyond what you can imagine or envision. Notice in the verse that it does not say "great people" but only great.

Now let's look at growing spiritually. *My question then is how can we grow spiritually? And my second question is what is spiritual growth?*

James 4:8 (KJV) says, "Draw nigh unto God, and he will draw nigh unto thee." Draw near to God. *How can you draw near to God?* Prayer and Bible study. We will look at both of these in a later session. *You cannot take either of these, prayer and Bible study, casually and grow spiritually. Do you agree or disagree with this statement, and why?*

What are the benefits of being close to God? You will gain or have wisdom, inner peace, discernment, and understanding of God's truth. *How are you going to know the truth without being close to God?* This comes through Bible study and prayer. Comment: A little knowledge is dangerous. A little biblical knowledge can be dangerous in that it can be misquoted out of context to fit a certain belief. Example: the woman caught in adultery. Or God is a God of love and would not send anyone to hell. We are going to look at this later in our study.

Now, I want to look at a couple of passages of scripture, and this is an area you may disagree with me, and that's okay. But *I want to see your thoughts on it and see how it can apply to spiritual maturity. Malachi 1:11–14 (NIV)* says:

> My name will be great among the nations, from the rising to the setting of the sun. In every place incense and pure offerings will be brought to my name, because my name will be great among the nations, says the LORD Almighty. But you profane it by saying of the Lord's table, 'it is defiled,' and of its food, 'It is contemptible.' And you say, 'What a burden,' and you sniff at it contemptuously, says the LORD Almighty. 'When

you bring injured, crippled or diseased animals and offer them as sacrifices, should I accept them from your hands?' says the LORD. 'Cursed is the cheat who has an acceptable male in his flock and vows to give it, but then sacrifices a blemished animal to the LORD. 'For I am a great king,' says the LORD Almighty, and my name is to be feared among the nations.'

Are we offering God our best when we are casual in our time of Bible study and prayer? We need to keep in mind that God is God, and He is to be reverenced. Can this passage be applied to our spiritual growth and maturity? Are we giving Him the best of our time and effort, or are we giving Him the injured, crippled, or diseased of our time?

Here is another passage, *Proverbs 3:9–10 (NIV)*: "Honor the LORD with your wealth, with the firstfruits of all your crops; then your barns will be filled to overflowing, and your vats will brim over with new wine." I know you are not supposed to change up scripture, but let's play with this. What if we make two changes and see how it can apply to our spiritual life? Honor the Lord with your wealth (heart), and with the firstfruits of your crops (life); then your barns will be filled to overflowing, and your vats will brim over with new wine. *Do you think that can have meaning in our walk with God?* Notice that we honor God first, then we receive the blessing. We are told to honor Him with our *first* fruits and with *all* our crops (life). We are to first be obedient, then God will fulfill His promises. Do not give God your leftovers and expect His blessings. Think what would happen in your life if you followed this verse.

To conclude this portion of our study, have you ever tried to have a discussion with someone about Jesus or faith and they respond, "My faith is private, between me and the Lord. I don't discuss it."

Do you agree or disagree with this statement, and why? "Your faith cannot be private. It must be shared."

- *What would your witness be like if you were private with your faith and never shared your belief?*

- *How could you properly teach and train up your children and grandchildren if you kept your faith private?*
- *How could you bring glory to God?*
- *Can you name anywhere in the Bible where God says keep His deeds, work, and blessings private?*

SESSION 2

Dealing with Sin

Who is your favorite Bible character and why? And you cannot name Jesus. Mine is David because his life was one battle after another. Isn't that what our life is like? If we are not in a trial or in a battle, get ready because it is about to happen. This is what life is about—fighting one battle after another.

So David was a man after God's own heart. What do we know about David? What are the major things we remember him for?

1. Goliath
2. Bathsheba
3. Warrior
4. King of Israel; shepherd who becomes king
5. Good or poor parent?
6. Wanted to build the temple
7. A man after God's own heart. *Why was David called a man after God's own heart? Acts 13:22 (NIV)* says, "After removing Saul, he made David their king. He testified concerning him; 'I have found David, son of Jesse, a man after my own heart; he will do everything I want him to do." *Because he will do everything I want him to do. We are going to look at the heart in the next session.*

Several of the things in David's life make us question how David could be considered a man after God's own heart. *Over the long haul, David sought to be righteous, and his heart's desire was to do God's will. He wanted to please God.*

So what can we learn from the weaknesses or sins David committed?

What is the first thing you think of when David is mentioned? I think most of us think of either Goliath or Bathsheba.

Let's look at Bathsheba and David's sin with her. First, one sin often leads to another—pride, lust, adultery, and murder to cover it up. Sin is progressive. And over time, sin becomes easier. You can lose your guilt of sin.

Think about this: one bad act, sin, can overshadow a lifetime of good. Let me show you.

What is the first thing you think of when you hear the name

1. *OJ Simpson;*
2. *Bill Clinton; and*
3. *Michael Jackson?*

What happens when we have sin in our life? Go to *Psalm 51* in your Bible, and look at David's life. Notice also how he responded.

- Verses 1–9: *What was David's life like? When we have sin in our life, do we have inner peace or turmoil? Where is our peace found? God is the God of peace, and Jesus is the Prince of Peace. Then how do we get peace with God?*
- Verses 10–11: confession, repentance, remorse
- Verse 12: restore the *joy* of your salvation. He had lost the joy of the Lord. Notice it does not say "restore my salvation." He never lost his salvation. He lost the joy and benefit of being close to God.
- Verses 15–17: What *does contrite mean?* Remorse, humble, to be crushed, and broken into pieces. *What would be the opposite of contrite?* Pride, arrogance, and being self-cen-

tered. *Often, we think it is sin for you but not for me because I am special. Pride, in my opinion, is the root of all sin.*

- Comment: We can be forgiven for our sins, but the consequences of our sin remain. Go in your Bible to *2 Samuel 12:11–18. What length of time was it from the time of David's sin until he was confronted by Nathan the prophet? What do you think David's life was like during this time? Do you think he had inner peace or turmoil?*

For another example of the effects of sin, let's look at the story about the prodigal son. This is located in *Luke 15:11–20* in your Bible.

What could wealth be, in addition to money and finances, that we could squander? Talents, time, gifts, reputation, and things entrusted to us. Remember when we looked at being a good steward and trustee?

What was the prodigal son's life like when he was with his father?

Look where sin takes the son in verses 14–16.

When he came to his senses—repentance—in verse 17.

Confession in verses 18 and 21.

Notice that the fellowship with the father was broken but not the relationship. *What does that mean to each of us?*

Recap: What are the effects of sin?

- One sin often leads to another sin, so sin is progressive.
- Sin becomes easier. Over time, you lose the guilt of sin.
- You can be forgiven for your sins, but the consequences of sin remain.
- Sin affects others, especially our family.
- You will have a broken *fellowship* with God but not a broken relationship. You will still be His child.
- Sin has a negative effect on us
  a) physically;
  b) mentally;
  c) emotionally;
  d) spiritually; and
  e) often financially.

Considering all of the effects of sin, why was David still considered a man after God's own heart after his sin? Look at David's heart as shown in *Psalm 40:8 (NIV):* "I desire to do your will, O my God; your law is within my heart." His desire was to be obedient to God. *This is the key to becoming a servant after God's own heart—obedience.*

I have often heard people say that they do not want to become a Christian because of all the "do this" or "do not do this" placed on their lives. *In other words, they refuse to make God the Lord of their life.* They want to be in control and do as they wish. *So my question is "Why did God give us the Ten Commandments?" What about His other laws, ordinances, statutes, and precepts? Are they given by God to restrict our lives?*

First John 4:7–8 (KJV) concludes with "God is love." *If God is truly a God of love, why would He want to restrict our lives with burdensome rules and regulations?* Actually, I think it is just the opposite. God wants to enhance our lives through His commandments, laws, ordinances, statutes, and precepts.

To illustrate this point, consider this example. Have you ever been traveling on a winding road in the hill country and you come upon a vehicle traveling at less than the speed limit? Maybe it is a truck or a recreational vehicle. Perhaps it is just someone out on a casual afternoon drive. You are in a hurry to get to your destination, and you are getting just a little aggravated. You keep trying to look past the vehicle in front of you, but every time you look, you see those yellow no-passing lines. Now you are thinking that all those cars you passed are going to catch up with you, and all the time you gained is being lost.

What is the purpose of the yellow no-passing lines? Are they not there to protect you and warn you of potential danger ahead? That is what God is trying to do with us when He gives us commandments, laws, ordinances, statutes, and precepts. *He is trying to enhance our lives, not restrict them.*

Let me try to show what I mean that God is enhancing our lives and not restricting them. Consider again the Ten Commandments from God (Exodus 20:1–17). *Can you state even one of the Ten Commandments that does not, in fact and practice, enhance our life? If we violate any of them, are there not consequences for our action? Do we have inner peace or turmoil?* If you steal something, do you not try to hide what you did and cover it up? If you commit adultery, are there not consequences to you and your family? When God said to honor the Sabbath and keep it holy, was God not telling us we need a day of rest to recharge our bodies and mind and to honor God? How about thou shalt have no other gods before me? It is true that you cannot serve two gods or masters, as stated in *Matthew 6:24 (NIV):* "No one can serve two masters. Either he will hate the one and love the other, or he will be devoted to the one and despise the other. You cannot serve both God and Money." *You are a servant to anything that masters you. You become a slave to it.* That is what ultimately happens when we covet something so much that it starts to dominate us, or we have sin that dominates us.

We could take each of the Ten Commandments, analyze them, and we would come up with the same result. God gave them to protect us and to enhance or build up our lives. He wants what is truly best for us.

Notice again the order of the Ten Commandments. Look where "Honor Thy Father and Mother" is located? *Do you think this is just a coincidence? Why? This anchors God to the family and the parents' role to lead and train up the children in the nurture and admonition of the Lord. The family is the basic unit of society, and the parents are to teach their children how to properly conduct themselves in society and their relationship with God.*

Look at what God says in *Psalm 19:7–11 (NIV):*

> The law of the LORD is perfect, reviving the soul.
> The statutes of the LORD are trustworthy, making
> wise the simple.
> The precepts of the LORD are right, giving joy to
> the heart.
> The commands of the LORD are radiant, giving
> light to the eyes.
> The fear of the LORD is pure, enduring forever.

The ordinances of the LORD are sure, and alto-
gether righteous. They are more precious than
gold, than much pure gold; they are sweeter than
honey, than honey from the comb.
By them is your servant warned; in keeping them
there is great reward.

If you will go back and slowly read each verse and carefully consider what it said, I think you will find how much God loves you and that He wants what is best for you. As He states in verse 11, He is warning us of dangers when we violate His instructions and guidance. And in keeping them, there is great reward. Our lives are enhanced. *God has a purpose and a reason behind everything He says and does.*

I think it is interesting that when God placed Adam in the garden of Eden, that He told him in *Genesis 2:16–17 (NIV)*, "And the LORD God commanded the man, 'You are free to eat from any tree in the garden; but you must not eat from the tree of the knowledge of good and evil, for when you eat of it you will surely die.'" This was God's first command to man. The tree of the knowledge of good and evil is forbidden fruit. *So the question is why did God command this to Adam?* Was it not to protect him and that there would be negative consequences if he ate from the tree?

Consider, again, the Ten Commandments and the consequences we suffer when we violate any of them. *Yes, there are consequences, and so often, they affect not only us individually but also our spouse and children, extended family, friends and relationships, our work, and numerous other areas of our life.* God is warning us that if we violate these principles, there will be negative consequences. *He is trying to protect us.*

This is why God commanded Adam not to eat of the tree of the knowledge of good and evil. He was trying to protect Adam from the consequences of eating the forbidden fruit. *God's intended purpose was to enhance Adam's life, not to place restrictions on Adam. (Whatever in our life that is the "the tree of knowledge of good and evil," we are to stay away from it, avoid it, and run from it. Do not even look at the temptation.)*

But let us not miss an important and vital part of what God stated in Genesis 2:16. Look again at the verse where it says, "You are free to eat from any tree in the garden." *This is the part we often overlook. We concentrate on what God says we cannot do or have instead of truly seeing what God says we can do and have!* God gave Adam all the trees in the garden of Eden to eat from, *except one and only one.* Consider all the different kinds of trees, fruit, nuts, avocados, olives, coconuts, pineapples, berries, etc. that God gave for Adam to eat from. *Think of how our lives would be enhanced if we concentrated on what God says we can do instead of what He commands we are not to do. God has given us an abundance of things to enjoy.* And in His wisdom, warns us of the things we are to avoid—things that are harmful to us.

Here's a thought for you. You can look for the bad in a matter or situation and you will find it, or you can look for the good in the same matter or situation and you will find it. Either way, you will find what you are looking for. In the matter above, one tree that is forbidden or numerous trees that are permitted and actually good for us.

Example: People who quit coming to church because "there are hypocrites at that church." *What are they looking for at the church, the good or the bad?*

Many people come to church looking for an *excuse* to quit coming instead of coming to worship God, to learn about Him and His ways, to enjoy the fellowship of other believers, and to grow spiritually. Notice I said *excuse* and not *reason. What is the difference between the two?* An excuse justifies your action, but it is not a fact. Whereas a reason is when your actions are based on fact.

A church member, who is a hypocrite, should not keep you from coming to church.

John 3:17 (KJV) says, "For God sent not his Son into the world to condemn the world, but that the world through him might be saved." Jesus came, out of God's love, to save but not to condemn. This is it! This is God's purpose! Think how it applies and correlates with and to all God has done to enhance and build up our lives.

Look at *John 10:10 (KJV):* "The thief cometh not but to steal, and to kill, and to destroy; I am come that they might have life, and that they might have it more abundantly." Jesus gives abundant life.

Satan kills, steals, and destroys. *What does sin (Satan) destroy?* He destroys your good name or reputation, family, career, health, influence, and finances.

Look again in your Bible to *Psalm 19:7–11* and see just how much God loves you and wants an abundant life for you.

Many years ago, I was teaching a Sunday school class. At the conclusion of the lesson, one of the members asked the question, "Are deathbed conversions fair?" His thought was that they had lived a life of earthly pleasures, then at the end of their life, they accept Jesus and go to heaven. I must admit I had thought this same thing before; however, this is the answer and response that I immediately had. No, they are not fair, and here is why. Look at all the benefits of following Jesus and being a servant of God that they have missed out on during their time on earth. I firmly believe that the Holy Spirit gave me that answer because I had never previously thought of it that way.

So here is my question for you to consider as we conclude this section of our study—what do you see? A life of restrictions or a life of enhancements? Do you see the one tree that is forbidden, or do you see all the other trees given for your enjoyment?

Guard Your Heart

In the context of this study—*becoming a servant after God's own heart—what does it mean to have a heart for God? What is "the heart" in our life?* I personally believe it includes several things—love, emotions, mental thinking (what fills your mind), character, passion (inner drive, intensity), the part of you that controls the issues of life—all of which lead to action or obedience.

Of these, let's look at three things.

Desire or passion for God

Psalm 42:1–2 (NIV) says, "As the deer pants for streams of water, so my soul pants for you, O God. My soul thirsts for God, for the living God. When can I go and meet with God?" My soul thirsts for the *living* God. Water is vital for survival. *Describe extreme thirst. What happens to you when you are dehydrated?* Fatigue, dizziness or light-headedness, confusion, headache, and low blood pressure.

Psalm 84:2 (NIV) says, "My soul yearns, even faints, for the courts of the Lord; for the living God; my heart and my flesh cry out for the living God."

What would your spiritual life be like without a thirst for God?

James 4:8 (KJV) tells us, "Draw nigh (near) to God, and he will draw nigh (near) to you." *Draw near to God. Can you name a better place to be than near to God? How do you draw near to God? We are going to look at this later.*

Love

Mark 12:28–31 (NIV) tells us:

> One of the teachers of the law came and heard them debating. Noticing that Jesus had given them a good answer, he asked him, "Of all the commandments, which is the most important?' 'The most important one," answered Jesus, 'is this: Hear, O Israel, the Lord our God, the Lord is one. Love the Lord your God with all your heart and with all your soul and with all your mind and with all your strength.

Love the Lord with *all your heart, soul, mind, and strength. What is missing—heart, soul, mind, strength? God covered everything—emotionally (heart), spiritually (soul), mentally (mind), and physically (strength). We are to love God with our "total" being. Love for the Lord and love for others.*

What is love for others? Care, concern, action, and compassion. Concern that leads to action. An example is the Good Samaritan. He had compassion, concern, taken action, and cared for his needs.

Proverbs 3:3–4 (NIV) says, "Let love and faithfulness never leave you; bind them around your neck, write them on the tablet of your heart. Then you will win favor and a good name in the sight of God and man." *Isn't this what God is looking for in a servant after His heart—love and faithfulness?*

Obedience

John 14:15, 21, 23–24 (NIV) tells us:

> "If you love me, you will obey what I command… Whoever has my commands and obeys

them, he is the one who loves me… Whoever has my commands and obeys them, he is the one who loves me. He who loves me will be loved by my Father, and I too will love him and show myself to him"…"Jesus replied, 'If anyone loves me, he will obey my teaching. My Father will love him, and we will come to him and make our home with him. He who does not love me will not obey my teaching. These words you hear are not my own; they belong to the Father who sent me."

Obedience is the key to spiritual growth and becoming a servant after God's own heart. We have studied David, king of Israel, and why he was considered a man after God's own heart from *Acts 13:22 (NIV):* "After removing Saul, he (God) made David their king. He testified concerning him; 'I have found David, son of Jesse, a man after my own heart; he will do everything I want him to do." Does this verse not state that David would do all God asked him to do, that David was obedient? Would this not be what is required from us to become a servant after God's own heart? *So the question is do you love Jesus enough to obey His commandments?*

Look at Proverbs 4:23. There are some interesting words in the three different translations:

> *Keep thy heart with all diligence: for out of it are the issues of life. (KJV)*

> *Watch over your heart with all diligence, For from it flow the springs of life. (Updated NASB)*

> *Above all else, guard your heart, for it is the wellspring of life. (NIV)*

In the KJV and the NASB, these verses state *diligence*, which means constant and steady in application. *We should have intense and constant effort when it comes to the spiritual condition of the heart.* The KJV also uses the word *keep*, which means to retain possession of, to have, the care of, to maintain, and to manage. We are to take care of our heart. The NIV uses the word *guard. If you guard something, you protect it from danger. This means to keep watch over your heart and take precautions to protect it.* Think of it in the context of the military. In the NASB, the word that stands out is *watch*. This means to have close observation of your heart or to be a watchman that protects and guards your heart. The NIV says "above all else"; this should be our first priority.

Notice that all of these provide some form of protection against danger. We are to be constant and steadfast in protecting our heart from anything that would harm our inner being and our relationship with God and with others. *Why does God instruct us to protect our heart? Because the heart determines how we respond to the issues we face in life.*

How do we guard or protect our heart?

Do your best to control (guard, protect) what your eyes see.

Do your best to control (guard, protect) what your ears hear.

Do your best to control (guard, protect) what goes into our mind.

Psalm 101:1–8 (NIV) is a good place to start:

> I will sing of your love and justice; to you, O Lord, I will sing praise, I will be careful to lead a blameless life—when will you come to me? I will walk in my house with blameless heart, I will set before my eyes no vile thing. The deeds of faithless men I hate; they will not cling to me. Men of perverse heart shall be far from me; I will have nothing to do with evil. Whoever slanders his neighbor in secret, him will I put to silence; whoever has haughty eyes and a proud heart, him will I not endure. My eyes will be on the faithful in the land, that they may dwell with me; he whose walk is blameless will minister to me. No one who practices deceit will dwell in my house;

no one who speaks falsely will stand in my presence. Every morning I will put to silence all the wicked in the land; I will cut off every evildoer from the city of the LORD.

Choose who you associate with wisely. You become like the people you associate with. *Proverbs 12:26 (NIV)* tells us, "A righteous man is cautious in friendship, but the way of the wicked leads them astray." *Why is this important in regard to guarding or protecting your heart?*

Proverbs 20:27 (NIV) says, "The lamp of the LORD searches the spirit of a man; it searches out his inmost being." Does God not search our spirit? Is our inmost being not our heart?

Looking again at Proverbs 4:23 (KJV). What are the "issues of life"?

- How you live.
- What you think about.
- How you respond to events, situations, and circumstances in life.
- What you believe.
- It is your character. *(You never know the true character of a person until their back is up against the wall). Comment: You can be legally right but morally wrong. Always choose what is morally right.*
- *How you react to adversity.*
- It is about what you treasure in your heart.
- It is about your relationship with God.
- It is about how you treat others, including your relationship with your wife and children.

Proverbs 27:19 (NIV) says, "As water reflects a face, so a man's heart reflects the man." The condition of the heart reflects or reveals the true character of a man.

Go to *Proverbs 13:11B*: "He who gathers money little by little makes it grow." Think how this could apply to our spiritual growth. It is not going to happen quickly. You should never stop growing spiritually. You will never get completely there spiritually. An example (may not be the best example) would be money and finances. When do you have enough? We can apply the principle of compounding here. You learn something and use it to build on something else. In this case, you are building or compounding your spiritual growth.

Throughout my forty-five-plus years in the financial industry, I had the honor and pleasure to work with people who were striving to achieve their dreams. *One of my natural tendencies is to ask why. Why do things happen the way they do, and in this case, why are some people successful and others are not? Are there common traits, qualities, or characteristics that successful people possess that those that are unsuccessful do not? Are the principles for success in the Bible, and if so, are they written for only select individuals, or are they for all to read and apply?*

What are some of the areas of life that the Bible gives guidance? It gives guidance in marriage, raising children, relationships, finances, and spiritual. Granted, there are many factors, events, and situations that can have a positive or negative effect on success. Some we can control and some of which we have absolutely no control. So my interest is in what we can control.

In my quest for the answer or key to success, I found two common characteristics in which most successful people possess and exercise. I believe both of these can be utilized by anyone if they are willing to work at them until they become a habit. *As we discuss these, consider how they can apply to us in becoming a servant after God's own heart and why they are important to spiritual growth. Actually, there is a third characteristic for spiritual growth—guard your heart—that we discussed earlier.*

So what are these two characteristics and can they be truly achieved by anyone dedicated to becoming a success and to growing spiritually?

Several years ago, I was one of the speakers at a consultants/small business owners meeting. I was told there were between 250 and 300 people in attendance. *I wanted my talk to be a combination of training, education, and motivation.*

I asked those in attendance to look around the room. Look to their right, then to their left, to those in front of them, and to those behind them. They were all consultants and business owners, and to some extent, competing for the same business. *I then asked a question: do you want your business/career to be better than theirs? Do you want to be better than your competition? Is there a secret to being a greater success than the individuals or companies that sell a similar product or service?*

In the context of this study, do you have competition in your pursuit of spiritual growth? Could your competition be yourself, in that your challenge is to grow each day? Comment: The greater the commitment, the greater the blessing. Something really special that I think you will realize when you grow spiritually is that you will start growing and strengthening other areas of your life—marriage, family, work, and church.

To answer the questions stated above about the characteristics of success, let's go to the Old Testament when God asked the young King Solomon what he would like for God to give him. From *2 Chronicles 1:10 (NIV)*, Solomon replied to God, "Give me wisdom and knowledge." Solomon said in *1 Kings 3:9 (NIV)*, "So give your servant a discerning heart." *To be successful in your career, business, and in your spiritual life, there is a critical, vital key and that is a constant pursuit of a heart for wisdom, knowledge, understanding, and discernment.*

In your pursuit of biblical wisdom, you must be smarter, better educated, and wiser than you were a month ago or a year ago. How can you become a success in something that you know little about? *To be successful in any area of life, you must continually educate yourself. It is a lifelong process to grow spiritually, little by little. Education, knowledge, and wisdom are the keys to being a success in any worthwhile endeavor.* If you read the book of Proverbs, notice how often the writer puts emphasis and value on the pursuit of wisdom, knowledge, understanding, and discernment. You gain a tremendous advantage when you are well trained and better educated. *This is how you become a godly influence on others, by knowing God's Word. How can you answer questions and share your faith without biblical knowledge?*

There is a story about a CEO of a company who was conducting a meeting with some of his senior staff members. The topic of the meeting was training. One of the staff members asked a question. "What if we spend the time and money training employees and they go to work for someone else? *Their new employer will get the benefit of our training.*"

The CEO's response was this. "What if we don't train them, and they stay? What is the cost?"

So my question is what is the cost of not educating yourself to grow spiritually?

I really like this statement: You will never go broke investing in yourself.

Proverbs 24:3–4 (NIV) states, "By wisdom [godly wisdom] a house [home, family] is built and through understanding it is established; through knowledge its rooms are filled with rare and beautiful treasures." Think how this verse applies to you and your spiritual growth—wisdom, understanding, knowledge, and discernment.

Proverbs 24:5 (NIV) says, "A wise man has great power, and a man of knowledge increases strength." *Wisdom is power, great power, and knowledge is strength.* Please do not miss this.

According to King Solomon, look at the impact wisdom and understanding can have on your life. *Proverbs 3:13–18 (NIV)* tells us:

> Blessed is the man who finds wisdom, the man who gains understanding, for she is more profitable than silver and yields better returns than gold. She is more precious than rubies, nothing you desire can compare with her. Long life is in her right hand; and in her left hand are riches and honor. Her ways are pleasant ways, and all her paths are peace. She is a tree of life to those who embrace her; those who lay hold of her will be blessed.

From these verses, what does wisdom bring? What are the benefits of wisdom? Blessings, long life, riches, honor, pleasant ways, peace, and nothing you desire can compare with wisdom. These are not my statements but are taken from the Word of God.

My great friend, who is an awesome Bible and Sunday school teacher, Rodney Richardson, shared an explanation about a verse of scripture with our class. The book of Proverbs was written "for attaining wisdom and discipline." This is taken from *Proverbs 1:1–2 (NIV):* "The proverbs of Solomon, son of David, King of Israel; for attaining wisdom and discipline' for understanding words of insight." *Rodney stated that the two go together and work together—wisdom and discipline. They make each other stronger and more powerful.* So we have studied wisdom as a principle for success; now we find our next key to success—self-discipline. The biblical word for discipline is *temperance. We will look at self-discipline in just a little bit.* Let's look at wisdom a little more and why it is important to our spiritual growth.

First, where do we start in our pursuit of godly wisdom?

From the verse in Proverbs 1:7 (NIV), "The fear of the LORD is the beginning of knowledge, but fools despise wisdom and discipline." *What does it mean to "fear" the Lord?* To reverence, honor, respect, and *letting God have the proper place in our lives. By not giving God the "leftovers or blemished sacrifices," as we studied earlier from Malachi chapter 1. We will need to keep Malachi chapter 1 in mind throughout this study.* This is the beginning or foundation of wisdom; *we are to build our lives on God and His teaching. And where do we learn about God?* From the Bible, God's Word. Between the Bible and the Holy Spirit, God has given you all you need for spiritual growth. This is how we draw near to God. From *James 4:8 (KJV),* "Draw nigh (near) to God and he will draw nigh (near) to you." *We get close to God by spending time in God's Word. Again, what better place is there than being near God?*

What are some steps for pursuing spiritual growth?

Step 1: Jesus. We are going to look at this in a later session.

Step 2: Deal with sin. We have discussed this.

Step 3: Bible study is vital for spiritual growth.

Step 4: A vibrant prayer life. Again, we will look at this in depth later in our study.

Step 5: Being discipled. *What does it mean to be discipled?* Discipled means to be a learner, to pursue godly wisdom.

Go to *Matthew 28:19–20 (NIV):* "Therefore go and make disciples of all nations, baptizing them in the name of the Father and of the Son and of the Holy Spirit, teaching them to obey everything I have commanded you. And surely, I am with you always, to the very end of the age."

How can you disciple or teach them if you do not have godly wisdom and biblical knowledge yourself? And where are you going to get this wisdom and knowledge? Through Bible study and guidance from the Holy Spirit.

God's Word will always be your main source for gaining spiritual nourishment and wisdom.

Determining to read through your Bible is a choice and a decision. Go to *Daniel 1:8 (NIV):* "But Daniel resolved not to defile himself with the royal food and wine." *Daniel* resolved. *What does it mean to be resolved?* It means to be determined, committed, to decide, or make a firm decision. I think this became Daniel's life. *How successful was Daniel's life?* We will go back to this verse several times throughout this study.

This means we will resolve to being committed to Bible study. I want to repeat something I said earlier—the greater the commitment, the greater the blessing. The greater the commitment to Bible study, the greater the blessing.

Comment: Do not fit God into your schedule. Fit your schedule into God. God should always be your priority.

So what can we do to make Bible study a strength in our spiritual growth? Set aside a time daily for Bible study. Make it a priority to be resolved. Do not give God your leftovers or blemished sacrifices, as we saw in Malachi 1. And *I believe it is important to* study *the Bible, not just read it.* This will take discipline—self-discipline or self-control.

I like to ask the following questions when I study the Bible:

- What is God's purpose in putting this in the Bible?
- Why was it important to God for Him to put this in the Bible?
- What is He trying to teach me?

- How can I apply this in my life?
- How is it to be used for the benefit of others?
- What is the truth from the passage of scripture? *Be careful not to take it out of context.* Often, you cannot take just one verse or passage of scripture and understand the full truth God intended. For instance, the story about the woman caught in adultery. People often use it in support of alternative lifestyles. What they leave out is the part where Jesus says, "Go and sin no more." He does not say it is okay to continue living in sin.
- Pray for godly wisdom, understanding, and insight. Look at *James 1:5 (NIV):* "If any of you lack wisdom, he should ask God, who gives generously to all without finding fault, and it will be given to him." We should continually pray for wisdom because life changes, circumstances change, situations change, and we face new trials and challenges.

Thought question: Is there a difference in having biblical wisdom and biblical knowledge? What is the difference? It is knowing how to *properly* understand and apply what the Bible says. Example: You can know about Jesus, but do you know Him as Lord and Savior?

Let's go back to *Proverbs 1:2 (NIV):* "For attaining wisdom and discipline; for understanding words of insight." For understanding words of insight relating to our knowledge of the Bible. Understanding means knowledge about a subject or situation, comprehension, a mental grasp of something, having insight or good judgment. In this case, the ability to grasp and comprehend the Word of God. To understand God's truth from the Bible.

This is further supported in *Proverbs 2:1–8 (NIV):*

> My son, if you accept my words and store
> up my commands within you, turning your ear
> to wisdom, and applying [application of God's
> Word] your heart to understanding, and if you
> call out for insight, and cry aloud for under-
> standing, and if you look for it as for silver, and

search for it as for hidden treasure, then you will understand the fear of the LORD, and find the knowledge of God. For the LORD gives wisdom [the source of wisdom], and from his mouth come knowledge and understanding. He holds victory in store for the upright, he is a shield to those whose walk is blameless, for he guards the course of the just, and protects the way of his faithful ones [verses 7 and 8 show the benefit of understanding.]

Comment: Knowledge without application is no better than not having knowledge. We need not only to read God's Word, but we need to understand it and apply it to and in our lives.

So we have studied wisdom as a principle for success; now we find our next key to success—self-discipline. The biblical word for discipline is *temperance.*

Self-discipline or self-control is the ability to make yourself do the things you do not want to do but deep down inside know you should. This applies to all areas of life—marriage, family, work, relationships, spiritual life, exercise, and finances. *Self-discipline or the ability to control oneself is a critical key to individual success.* Deep down inside, everybody knows what he or she should do. *They know what is right and wrong, what is moral and immoral, what is good for you and what is bad, what builds up and what tears down. (When you yield to your emotions over your good judgment, you lack self-discipline.)*

What does the Bible say about self-discipline? Proverbs 25:28 (KJV) states, "He that hath no rule over his own spirit is like a city that is broken down, and without walls." If we look back at biblical times when this verse of scripture was written, cities built walls for protection. *God is telling us that if we do not control ourselves and we do not exercise self-discipline, we are without protection. We are exposed to danger.* We are weak when we do not use self-discipline; just like when the city did not have walls, it was weak and exposed to danger. *Remember earlier when we discussed guarding your heart. It takes self-discipline to guard and protect your heart!*

Motivational writer Napoleon Hill says, "If you do not conquer yourself, you will be conquered by yourself."

Another scripture over self-discipline is *1 Corinthians 9:25–27 (KJV)*:

> And every man that striveth [strive—to try hard, to make an intense effort] for the mastery [superiority] is temperate [or has self-control] in all things. [Everyone that strives to be superior in all things has self-control], Now they do it to obtain a corruptible crown but we, an incorruptible [we do it for spiritual growth, in the case of this study]. I, therefore, so run, not as uncertainly [uncertainly—not knowing where you are going or what to do. I know where I am going]; so fight I [we are engaged in the fight], not as one that beateth the air [shadow boxing, not being engaged in the fight, but pretending to be]; But I keep under my body, and bring it into subjection [I exercise self-discipline. I am going to take control of my body, my actions, my thoughts], lest that by any means, when I have preached to others, I myself should be a castaway.

What is a castaway? A castaway is someone without friends or resources. If you do not master yourself and exercise self-discipline, you will be without friends or resources.

What are some areas of life where we need self-control or self-discipline? Areas such as work, marriage, relationships, exercise, diet, and finances. *Where do we need self-discipline in our spiritual life?* In our Bible study, prayer life, church, service or caring for others, and stewardship (and this could include multiple things—finances, family, abilities, talents, and gifts).

A little sacrifice, self-discipline; today is much better than a lot of regret tomorrow. *This actually means we have two choices when it comes to self-discipline. We can choose to discipline ourselves and have the pain of sacrifice and growth for a short period of time, or we can choose to give in to short-term pleasure and suffer the pain of regret later, as well as the related consequences.* Each of us must choose which path we will follow, and we will reap the rewards or suffer the consequences according to our decisions. *Remember this—you are a slave to anything that masters or controls you.*

Now, I want to look at several verses of scripture pertaining to self-control. There are several, but there is a point I want to make as we look at each verse. Think about who the author or writer is of each book:

> Be *self-controlled* and alert. Your enemy the devil prowls around like a roaring lion looking for someone to devour. *(1 Peter 5:8 NIV; emphasis mine)*

> For this very reason, make every effort to add to your faith goodness; and to goodness; knowledge; and to knowledge; *self-control'* and to self-control; perseverance; and to perseverance; godliness, and to godliness; brotherly kindness; and to brotherly kindness; love. For if you possess these qualities in increasing measure, they will keep you from being ineffective and unproductive in your knowledge of our Lord Jesus Christ. *(2 Peter 1:5–8 NIV; emphasis mine)*

> Do not deprive each other except by mutual consent and for a time, so that you may devote yourselves to prayer. Then come together again so that Satan will not tempt you because of your lack of *self-control*. *(1 Corinthians 7:5 NIV; emphasis mine)*

> Now the overseer must be above reproach, the husband of but one wife, temperate, *self-con-*

trolled, respectable, hospitable, able to teach, not given to drunkenness, not violent but gentle, not quarrelsome, not a lover of money. *(1 Timothy 3:2–3 NIV; emphasis mine)*

For God did not give us a spirit of timidity, but a spirit of power, of love and of *self-discipline. (2 Timothy 1:7 NIV; emphasis mine)*

But mark this; There will be terrible times in the last days. People will be lovers of themselves, lovers of money, boastful, proud, abusive, disobedient to their parents, ungrateful, unholy, without *self-control*, brutal, not lovers of the good, treacherous, rash, conceited, lovers of pleasure rather than lovers of God—having a form of godliness but denying its power. Have nothing to do with them. *(2 Timothy 3:1–5 NIV; emphasis mine)*

For the grace of God that brings salvation has appeared to all men. It teaches us to say "No" to ungodliness and worldly passions, and to live *self-controlled*, upright, and godly lives in this present age. *(Titus 2:11–12 NIV; emphasis mine)*

But the fruit of the Spirit is love, joy, peace, patience, kindness, goodness, faithfulness, gentleness, and *self-control*. Against such things there is no law. *[Self-control is one of the fruit or produce of the Holy Spirit, what the Holy Spirit produces in each of us.] (Galatians 5:22–23 NIV; emphasis mine)*

Blessed are the meek, for they will inherit the earth." *[What do we normally think of when someone is called meek?* That they are easy to control or manipulate, a pushover. Note that meek is also listed as a fruit of the Spirit. *My research shows humble, gentle, strength under control, power to resist, and restraint. Would this not be self-control or self-discipline?]* (Matthew 5:5 NIV)

Poverty and shame will come to him who neglects discipline. *(Proverbs 13:18 NASB)*

He who neglects discipline despises himself. *(Proverbs 15:32 NASB)*

Here is the point I want to make. Look at all the different books of the Bible we read in the verses above, many with different authors, that all stressed the importance of the ability to control ourselves. Authors from both the Old and New Testaments. *Does this not show the importance of exercising self-control?*

Can you think of any area of life where self-discipline is not important and necessary?

I was asked one time—how do you get self-discipline if you do not have it? It is like obtaining any other skill; you have to practice it. Take those areas of weakness and just make yourself do them until it becomes a habit. Yes, that's right. To get self-discipline, you have to practice self-discipline.

One final thought on self-discipline. We are studying the life of David, king of Israel. *Would David's life have been different, for the better or worse, if he had exercised self-discipline with Bathsheba? How about the life of his children? How about Bathsheba and Uriah?*

How about the prodigal son that we looked at earlier? How would his life have been different if he had exercised self-control?

Some of the keys to spiritual growth are

- guard your heart;
- pursue godly wisdom; and
- exercise self-control.

Four Incredible Gifts from God

I was attending a church social some time ago, and the question was asked, "If you could, would you go back in time or would you go forward in time?" Just for fun, let us go back in time. *What was the best gift you received from someone?* Maybe you've had several gifts that were all very special to you. It was possibly a gift at Christmas, birthday, anniversary, or special occasion. It could have been something special that someone did for you at a time in your life that you really needed the gift. Perhaps the gift was financial, giving counsel or advice, or it was giving comfort or support in a time of great need. That is a great thing about gifts in that they can be multiple things— some tangible, some are acts of kindness, or counsel at a critical time of your life.

Now let us look at the giving of gifts from a different view. *Consider a time when you gave someone a special gift that they really wanted or needed; how did it make you feel to give them that gift?* If I am correct, many times and probably most of the time, the giver of great gifts receives the most pleasure from the exchange. *Why did you give that special gift?* I personally believe that when we are the giver of these awesome gifts, there is one key and common characteristic—love.

So as we consider the giving or receiving of special, thoughtful gifts, what if the receiver refuses to accept the gift? There is no benefit to either party. The receiver walked away empty-handed. The giver probably walked away brokenhearted.

Or the recipient did not show any appreciation for the gift? They just placed it on a shelf or in the closet and left it there or showed no interest in it whatsoever. *How would you feel?*

Let me give you an example. When you were dating your wife and you came to the time you wanted to ask her to marry you and you wanted to buy her an engagement ring, you wanted it to be really special. You love her with all your heart, so you spent time and effort to find the perfect ring just for her. You planned the best time to ask her. You got down on one knee and showed her the ring; you asked her to marry you, and she turned you down. She said she just wants to be "casual" friends and see each other occasionally, maybe on holidays or special events like Easter or Christmas. *How do you feel?*

With that thought, the topic I would like to explore are the gifts that God gives us, His children. There are so many things I could include, but I want to focus on what I believe are His four greatest gifts to us. As we look at these four gifts, *let us consider not only the gifts but also why God gave each particular gift. What was God's purpose in the giving of each one?* All of these gifts take in the total character of God, including but not limited to God being holy, righteous, and just, as well as a God of love. And it is because of His great love for us that He gives us these gifts. The four gifts all work together as a whole and complete and complement each other. In fact, *these are gifts that only God can give. You cannot get them from any other source. And they are fundamental to becoming a servant after God's own heart. Accordingly, each one should be treasured and never taken casually.* Please grasp what I have just said. *Because these gifts from God are so unique and special, they should be revered and cherished.* When God does something, He does it in a great and mighty way that always brings glory and praise to Him. God offers these gifts to each of us, but we all, individually, must decide if we will accept His loving and gracious gifts, not just at Easter or Christmas but every day.

This is what I would like for you to remember and concentrate on as we look at each of these four invaluable gifts from God. *Each of them has great value and should not be taken casually or lightly in the life of the believer.* They are to be a part of our daily discipline for our spiritual growth. God has given each of them to us for our individual benefit. Please do not miss how much each of us need these gifts. They are so vital and of great importance, just as you need air to breathe, food to eat, and water to drink. They are necessary for our spiritual survival, and we are to accept each gift that God has given us. We must utilize and apply them in our lives for our individual benefit and well-being, so we can have His abundant life, not only on this earth but also for eternity with God in heaven. Jesus says in *John 10:10 (KJV)*, "I am come that they might have life, and that they might have it more abundantly."

What does it mean to you, individually, to have abundant life in Jesus?

Now is the time for us to open and study these gifts that are so special and unique that only God can give them and hopefully realize how great God's love is for us. I intentionally waited to name the gifts because I was concerned that you would see them and think they were too obvious and dismiss my passion in sharing their awesome value to us. *James 1:17 (NIV)* states, "*Every* good and perfect gift is from above, coming down from the Father of the heavenly lights." So the good and perfect gifts from God are Jesus and through Him the gift of eternal life with Him in heaven, the gift of the Holy Spirit, the gift of God's Holy Bible, and the gift of prayer. Now we can delve into each of these gifts and why God gave them to His children. *And I want to remind you that each of these gifts maintain the total character of God—He is holy, righteous, just, and pure, as well as love.*

This section is the heart and soul of this study of becoming a servant after God's own heart. It is the meat and potatoes; the backbone, if you will. It has application in all the other areas, and they are built around this part of our study.

Jesus

Several years ago, I was a part of a three-man Bible study. We were neighbors, and we met together once a week. One of the men grew up in the Catholic faith; however, he was not a practicing Catholic. As we progressed in the Bible study, my Catholic friend kept making the statement that there had to be more than one way to heaven than faith in Jesus. The only response I could think of was to show me in the Bible where it states there is more than one way.

How would you have responded to my Catholic friend?

Probably the most well-known verse of scripture is *John 3:16 (KJV):* "For God so loved the world, that he gave his only begotten Son, that whosoever believeth in him should not perish, but have everlasting life." This is the first verse of scripture that most of us memorized as a child. *This verse clearly states God's purpose and why He gave this gift to us.* There are some key theological facts stated in this passage. "For God so loved the world" tells us why God gave us the gift of Jesus. Because He loves us. And because of His love for us, He *gave* His one and only begotten Son, Jesus. He gave His Son. It is a gift and not something we have earned, purchased, or achieved. We become God's child when we accept Jesus as Lord and Savior. But Jesus is God's only begotten Son, conceived by the Holy Spirit.

What are some ways, besides Jesus, that people try to use to go to heaven?

If our salvation could be earned, purchased, or achieved, why did Jesus have to go to the cross to redeem us from the penalty of our sins? Salvation would no longer be a gift from God but would be obtained by our own effort. *If it could be purchased, what would be the price? Would that mean only rich people could go to heaven?* That is certainly not supported by scripture. *What could we offer God that is not already His?* All of these would result in pride and self-achievement. Pride makes it about self and not about God. *If salvation came by doing good deeds, how would you know when you had done enough? What would be acceptable good deeds and what would not qualify? Is there a level of deeds you could do to earn your way to heaven? If you sinned, would that take away your salvation, and you would have to "re-earn" your way to heaven? And how would personal effort maintain the total character of God?*

Continuing to look at John 3:16, we see that God so loved the world. That would be you and me, as well as all of mankind, from beginning to end. He has made the ultimate gift of Jesus available to anyone who will accept it. It breaks God's heart for those who refuse.

It has been often said that God is a God of love and that He would not send anyone to hell. How would you respond to that statement? My response to that is that God loves us so much that He provided the pathway to heaven, Jesus, His only begotten Son, which is further supported in John 3:16, whosoever believeth in Him. Anyone who goes to hell is because they refused to accept Jesus as Lord and Savior. This is the ultimate gift that only God could give.

Why would God do this for us? Love—absolutely. But also so that we could spend eternity with Him in heaven. That we would have everlasting life, as stated in John 3:16. *How would you describe eternity?* The terms *eternity* and *everlasting* mean time without end. This is a difficult concept for our human minds to accept. Virtually everything known to man ultimately has an end or expiration. *Eternity is time without end, being spent either in heaven or hell, with the decision being left up to each of us individually to decide where we will spend eternity.*

If we look at the final part of 1 John 4:8, it very simply says, "For God is love." *What are the other characteristics of God, or how would you describe God?* Yes, He is a God of love, but love is only one characteristic of God. He is also holy, righteous, just, and pure. Absolutely *God loves us, but we are to also love Him in return.* The thought that God loves us and would not send anyone to hell *implies God is to love us, but what about our love of God?* Can any relationship be built on one person showing love and compassion and the other never returning love?

Look at the other characteristics of God. To be holy is to be morally perfect, divine, and sacred; righteous is to be just, upright, and doing what is right; and pure is untainted, spotless, blameless, chaste, and innocent. If we look at the total character of God, He is love, morally perfect, sacred, just, upright, untainted, spotless, blameless, and innocent. *How can God maintain and accept anything less than these characteristics in heaven and still maintain His character in total?* Heaven would no longer be morally perfect, divine, sacred, just, upright, pure, untainted, spotless, blameless, and innocent. *Love would still be there, but all else would be diluted and impure.*

Some have said that Christians are intolerant for believing that Jesus is the only way to heaven. *Do you think Christians are being intolerant for believing this?* I personally believe that it is love that motivates us to believe this. If God, Jesus, and the Bible are all a myth and Christians strive to live their lives according to Jesus's teaching, what have they lost? Does not any good that they have done throughout their lives, in the name of God, contribute to the betterment of others and society? But what if the Bible and Jesus are true, that heaven and hell are real, and we will in fact spend eternity at one place or the other? Are Christians' not showing love and concern for their fellow man by not wanting anyone to spend eternity in hell rather than being intolerant?

That brings us to this question. Why Jesus? Why is Jesus the way and the truth and the life, and no one comes to the Father except through Him (Jesus), as stated in *John 14:6*, and further supported by *Romans 10:9–10 (NIV)*: "That if you confess with your mouth, 'Jesus is Lord,' and believe in your heart that God raised him from the dead, you will be saved. For it is with your heart that you believe and are justified, and it is with your mouth that you confess and are saved."

Why, then, is Jesus the only way? Why not another path to heaven? I believe this goes back to what I just stated about God's total character and maintaining His total character in heaven. God loves us, and He deeply desires that we all spend eternity with Him in heaven. *Second Peter 3:9 (NIV) states, "The Lord is not slow in keeping his promise, as some understand slowness. He is patient with you, not wanting anyone to perish, but everyone to come to repentance."* As I stated above, eternity is defined as endless or infinite time. There is no end to eternity. I believe everyone will spend eternity in either heaven or hell. Hell is described as a place of eternal misery, torture, and torment.

The requirement of a sacrifice to redeem us from the penalty of our sins. The sacrifice must be without blemish. *Deuteronomy 17:1 (NIV)* states, "Do not sacrifice to the LORD your God an ox or a sheep that has any defect or flaw in it, for that would be detestable to him."

The atonement is in the blood. *Leviticus 17:11 (NIV)* says, "For the life of a creature is in the blood, and I have given it to you to make atonement for yourselves on the altar; it is the blood that makes atonement for one's life."

Atonement means to pay the price, to be reconciled, redemption, and to make amends for a wrong.

Jesus was the sacrifice for our sins and He was without blemish and He shed His blood as atonement for our sins.

Christ is the acceptable sacrifice. *Hebrews 4:15 (NIV)* says, "For we do not have a high priest who is unable to sympathize with our weaknesses, but we have one who has been tempted in every way—just as we are—yet was without sin."

Hebrews 10:10 (NIV) tells us, "We have been made holy through the sacrifice of the body of Jesus Christ once for all." It is final, once for all. There is no need to do it again.

Hebrews 9:22 (NIV) states, "Without the shedding of blood there is no forgiveness." The cross and Jesus's blood provides the forgiveness of sin and gives the atonement for our transgressions.

Second Corinthians 5:21 (NIV) says, "God made him who had no sin to be sin for us, so that in him we might become the righteousness of God." *Holiness and righteousness are necessary to enter heaven, and they are found only through faith in Jesus as your Lord and Savior.*

Since God loves us and wants each of us to be with Him in heaven for eternity, sinful man needs to be redeemed and made spotless and righteous. To accomplish this, we need a Redeemer or sacrifice to redeem us from the penalty of our tainted and impure life.

With God being the only thing holy, righteous, just, and pure, He Himself was the ONLY *acceptable Redeemer or sacrifice. A sacrifice is to give up something of great value. If it, the sacrifice, does not have great value, then it is not truly a sacrifice.* He (God) came to earth in the form of His only begotten Son, Jesus. And Jesus, on the cross, became our Redeemer and Savior. *When we place our faith in Jesus as Lord and Savior, God clothes us with the righteousness of Jesus.* He covers us with His (Jesus) righteousness. *First Corinthians 1:30 (NIV)* states, "It is because of him, that you are in Christ Jesus, who has become for us wisdom from God—that is, our righteousness, holiness, and redemption." *This is what makes us acceptable to enter heaven. Jesus is our righteousness, holiness, and redemption. To state again, 2 Corinthians 5:21 (NIV)* tell us, "God made him [Jesus], who had no sin to be sin for us; so that in him [Jesus] we might become the righteousness of

God." *(Jesus provides the righteousness or purity we need to be able to enter heaven, and the character of God is maintained and preserved in heaven.)*

Question: (Can you think of a better way or plan to heaven and God retains His character?) Can you think of a greater sacrifice than God's only begotten Son? What other way could there be? What other sacrifice would be acceptable?

Please grasp all this about God's great and awesome gift that He has offered to us in His only begotten Son, Jesus Christ. This shows how much God loves us. *Only God can give the gift of Jesus.*

The Holy Spirit

I was sitting in a Sunday school class many years ago, and the teacher made the comment that the only role of the Holy Spirit was to convict us of sin. I knew that was wrong, so I said that is not true. However, at that time, I was unable to think of the facts that proved him wrong. The Holy Spirit has multiple duties. *This incredible gift from God is actually God's Spirit living in each of His children. This amazes me.* This is how much God loves us, and it shows how important we are to Him. *Why would God do this, place His Holy Spirit in each of His believers?* What is His purpose? He knew we would continually be under attack from Satan and be tempted to sin. God knew we would need His presence, not only at our acceptance of Jesus as Savior but also throughout our lifetime to guide and assist us in our daily walk with Him.

As we look at the incredible gift from God, the Holy Spirit, let us consider first who God is. He is the Creator of the heavens and the earth, everything on earth, the universe, the sun, the moon, and the stars. God is the Supreme Being. He is King of kings and Lord of lords. There is none greater than God. Step back for a minute and try to realize who God is and all that it involves.

The Holy Spirit is a part of the Trinity—God the Father, Jesus (Redeemer), and the Holy Spirit, God living in us, His children (let that soak in; the Holy Spirit is God living in us)—with each member of the Trinity performing a different role in the spiritual life of the believer.

This is what *1 Corinthians 6:19–20 (NIV)* says about the Holy Spirit: "Do you not know that your body is a temple of the Holy Spirit, who is in you, whom you have received from God? You are not your own; you were bought at a price. Therefore, honor God with your body." God's Spirit lives in us and is there to continually guide and direct our lives.

As we consider why God gave us the gift of the Holy Spirit, look at how God enriches and enhances us through the amazing work and activity of the Spirit in our lives and try to realize how much God loves us.

Now let us explore this incredible gift God has given us in the Holy Spirit and the role the Spirit plays in the life of each believer. *As we study each function of the Holy Spirit, note again that these are things only God can do.*

Comforter. John 14:15–18 (KJV) states:

> If ye love me, keep my commandments. And I will pray the Father, and he shall give you another Comforter, that he may abide with you forever; Even the Spirit of Truth, whom the world cannot receive, because it seeth him not, neither knoweth him; but ye know him; for he dwelleth with you, and shall be in you. I will not leave you comfortless; I will come to you.

There are several things this passage of scripture tells us. First, Jesus said He will pray to the Father for God to give the Spirit of truth, the comforter. That would mean it is a gift from God. *The Spirit of truth reveals God's truth, as opposed to Satan's lies and deception. Second, that the Spirit dwells or lives in those of us who know and have faith in Him, Jesus, and that he may abide with you forever.* Third, He is our comforter. We may be able to get some comfort or peace from family, friends, or members of the clergy, but the comfort and peace that passes all understanding can only come from God, through the work of the Holy Spirit.

Gives spiritual gifts. First Corinthians 12:7–11 (NIV) states:

> Now to each one the manifestation of the Spirit is given for the common good. To one there is given through the Spirit the message of wisdom, to another the message of knowledge by means of the same Spirit, to another faith by the same Spirit, to another gifts of healing by that one Spirit, to another miraculous powers, to another prophecy, to another the distinguishing between spirits, to another speaking in different kinds of tongues, and to still another the interpretation of tongues. All these are the work of one and the same Spirit, and he gives them to each one, just as he determines.

The Holy Spirit provides each believer with gifts, talents, or abilities that are to be used in our individual ministries for the benefit of others and God's glory—just as he determines. *One of the greatest things God tells us to do is to take care of each other—to do things that will build up and not tear down and things for the common good.*

Look at what the Holy Spirit does to prepare or equip the believers for and in their individual ministries. *Ephesians 4:11–13 (NIV)* says:

> It was he who gave some to be apostles, some to be prophets, some to be evangelists, and some to be pastors and teachers, *to prepare God's people for works of service*, so that the body of Christ may be built up until we all reach unity in the faith and in the knowledge of the Son of God, and become mature, attaining to the whole measure of the fullness of Christ. (emphasis mine)

The Holy Spirit equips each believer for their areas of ministry or service for the building up of the church and each other. We are not alone in our individual ministries or service to build up the kingdom of God. He gives us, through the Holy Spirit, what we need in our areas of service.

Do you remember my definition of success? Becoming the person that God wants you to be and being a good steward of the gifts, talents, abilities, and opportunities He gives you. *This is done by allowing the Holy Spirit to work in us and through us.*

The fruit of the Spirit. Galatians 5:22–23 (NIV) tells us, "But the fruit of the Spirit is love, joy, peace, patience, kindness, goodness, faithfulness, gentleness, and self-control. Against such things there is no law."

Fruit is the product of a seed planted, nurtured, and properly cared for. As we look at the fruit of the Spirit, *are any of these not for our benefit and for the good of others?* This is what happens when we live a Spirit-filled life. Our life is enhanced and the lives of others are as well, and we bear, yield, and produce the fruit of the Spirit.

Guidance. John 16:13 (NIV) says, "But when he, the Spirit of truth, comes, he will guide you into all truth."

He will guide you in spiritual truth. Many people today quote passages from the Bible without searching the Scriptures for biblical truth. They make statements about what the Bible says to support their individual causes and may be taken out of context. But you should have spiritual discernment, guidance, and understanding to state biblical truth. This can only come through the guidance of the Holy Spirit and intense Bible study.

Our counselor, teacher, and helper. John 14:26 (NIV) states, "But the Counselor, the Holy Spirit, whom the Father will send in my name, will teach you all things and will remind you of everything I have said to you."

Can you think of a better teacher than the Holy Spirit? God, the Creator of the heavens and the earth and all that is within them, being our counselor, teacher, and helper. Does this not show how much God loves us?

Reveals Jesus. In *John 15:26 (NIV)*, Jesus said, "When the Counselor comes, whom I will send to you from the Father, the Spirit of truth who goes out from the Father, he will testify about me."

It is through the work of the Holy Spirit that we each individually come to accept Jesus as our personal Lord and Savior and accept Him as the Redeemer for the penalty of our sins. The Holy Spirit reveals Jesus to us and convicts us of our sins.

Resides in us. First Corinthians 6:19–20 (NIV) says, "Do you not know that your body is the temple of the Holy Spirit, who is in you, whom you have received from God? You are not your own; you were bought at a price. Therefore, honor God with your body."

The Holy Spirit is in each of us who are God's children and is with us at all times. He is there to guide, counsel, help, assist, and discipline us. *Why would God do this?* God does this because of His great love for us.

Intercedes for us in prayer. Romans 8:26–27 (NIV) tells us:

> The Spirit helps us in our weakness. We do not know what we ought to pray for, but the Spirit himself intercedes for us with groans that words cannot express. And he who searches our hearts knows the mind of the Spirit, because the Spirit intercedes for the saints in accordance with God's will.

We may not know or understand God's will for us, but the Holy Spirit knows and intercedes for us in prayer. God knows us even better than we know ourselves. And He also knows what our future holds. Isn't it awesome that the Holy Spirit intercedes with the Father for each of us, God's children? Please grasp the love of God in this and the impact the Holy Spirit has on our lives.

Our salvation is sealed by the Holy Spirit. A seal is a guarantee, testimony, confirmation, and assurance that it is a fact, and it is binding. *Ephesians 1:13–14 (NIV)* states:

> And you also were included in Christ when you heard the word of truth, the gospel of your

> salvation. Having believed, you were marked in him with a seal, the promised Holy Spirit, who is a deposit guaranteeing our inheritance until the redemption of those who are God's possession—to the praise of his glory. [Also, from *2 Corinthians 1:22, 5:5 and Ephesians 4:30.*]

In this case, seal means to establish or determine something is irrevocable, to prove accuracy or quality, or that it is authentic. *The Holy Spirit guarantees and confirms our salvation is true and that it is irrevocable and authentic.* This shows the validity of once saved, always saved—the seal of the Holy Spirit. Only believers are sealed by the Holy Spirit. This happens when we accept Jesus as Lord and Savior, and the Holy Spirit comes to dwell in us and *His presence in us is the seal of God that we are saved. The Holy Spirit is God, and there is none greater than God, so God Himself seals our redemption.*

As we consider the role of the Holy Spirit, think about what holy means. Holy is being sacred, set aside or separate, and reserved for God and His divine purpose. Accordingly, the Holy Spirit should be greatly respected and reverenced. *We should not be complacent with this gift that only God can give.*

The Holy Bible

The next amazing gift from God we want to discuss is the Holy Bible. Notice again the word holy. It is called the Holy Bible because it is, in fact, sacred and reserved for God and His divine purposes.

The Holy Bible is another incredible gift showing how much God loves us. God pours out His love for us so much that *the Bible should not be read like any other book.* When you read and study the Bible, you should search it for *God's truth* and pray not to be deceived by Satan and worldly teachings. Each time you study the Bible, you should ask, "What is God's purpose and His will in putting this in the Bible? What is God trying to teach me through this passage of scripture? And what is the biblical truth in what I am reading?"

Follow with me God's purpose in the gift of the Bible as stated in *2 Timothy 3:16–17 (KJV)*: "All scripture is given by inspiration of God, and is profitable for doctrine, for reproof, for correction, for instruction in righteousness. That the man of God may be perfect, thoroughly furnished unto all good works." *From this verse, what are some of God's purposes in the Bible?* This says that *all* scripture is inspired by God, and His purpose is to teach, correct, and train His children in the way that they should live and so that we can do good works, as the scripture states. Accordingly, reading and studying the Bible is absolutely vital for spiritual growth. In verse 15 of that chapter, it says that the scriptures are to "make you wise for salvation through faith in Christ Jesus." The Bible points to Jesus as the way for salvation.

What are some things that make the Bible the uniquely inspired Word of God?

Here are some thoughts I find interesting in support of the Holy Bible being the inspired Word of God:

- The Bible carries the same theme throughout—God's love and redemption from sin through faith in Jesus.
- The time frame in which the entire Bible was written spans approximately 1,500 years, according to the commentary in my King James Version.
- There are forty different authors of the sixty-six books in the Bible, and all their writings are interwoven and weaved together with the same prophesy, theme, facts, and give support to the total character of God. *Only God could do this.*
- Each chapter of the Bible is numbered, as well as each verse of the scriptures. This allows us to easily identify, locate, reference, and cross-reference passages of scriptures. I do not know of any other book written like this.
- This is a personal observation about the Bible being inspired by God. Moses wrote the book of Genesis. But Moses was not alive during the time of creation or Adam and Eve. *How did Moses know these facts if they were not*

given to him by God? How did Moses know about the six days God created and rested on the seventh? How could these facts have been recorded for Moses to know about them?

- The Word of God, the Holy Bible, has stood the test of time. *What was truth, when it was written, is still truth today. What was sin, when it was written, is still sin today, regardless of what man, politicians, or judges may say.*

- Consider how many times in the Old Testament that a verse says, "Thus sayeth the Lord" or "the word of the Lord."

- The Bible is the ONLY Book that was written especially and specifically for YOU—and ME—individually and collectively. All of the passages in the Bible were written to enrich our lives—AND THEY WORK.

- The Bible is full of scripture relating to money and finance, parenting, marital relationships, work and work ethic, and so much more. God, through the scriptures, teaches us how to deal with stress and the trials and tribulations we face in life. These are all life issues that God addresses in His Word. He is trying to enhance our lives to give us life more abundantly.

- The Bible is filled with numerous prophecies, many of which have already been fulfilled. Some of them came about even during our lifetime—*exactly as God stated in His Word.*

- Have you ever read a verse of scripture and thought, *Now that is a really interesting thought.* Here is one for you to think about concerning this incredible gift from God. *Psalm 34:8 (NIV)* says, "Taste and see that the LORD is good." Exactly what is God saying to us when He says "taste and see"? When you taste something, it means you have to eat it to taste it, but eating it gets the food inside you and that is where you receive the benefit. I think what God is saying to us is that we should love Him so much that we have a hunger and thirst for Him and His Word. *Matthew 5:6 (NIV)* reads, "Blessed are those who hunger and thirst for righteousness, for they will be filled." Few things in life affect us more than being hungry or thirsty. We must eat and drink to survive. They are necessities for life. Notice the result of having a hunger and thirst for righteousness; we will be filled.

If you go to a grocery store and look around at all the food, how much does all that food benefit you if you walk out of the store without purchasing any of it? Even if you purchase some fruit, vegetables, and meat, you still receive no benefit until you actually eat the food. That is when you get it inside you and that is when it is beneficial. This is how it is with the Word of God; you have to get it inside you to get any benefit.

Another way to illustrate this would be if you wanted to learn how to play a musical instrument. If you intend to play an instrument and play it well, you must study music, take lessons, and spend many hours in practice. You do not just sit down one day and start to play. It takes time and a lot of effort. What happens if you quit playing for an extended, lengthy period of time? Your skills deteriorate. It is the same with your spiritual growth. It deteriorates without being utilized. Accordingly, we must read and study God's Word to continue to grow spiritually.

Another thought is that you must do it yourself. No one else can do it for you, just like playing a musical instrument.

That is the way it is in getting to truly know God. You have to spend time with Him, and it is an ongoing process. It is a lifetime commitment.

So go ahead and take a taste. Then continue to enjoy the banquet God has placed before you. Taste and see that all of God's Word is written for our benefit and spiritual nourishment, as stated in *Proverbs 10:3 (NIV):* "The LORD does not let the righteous go hungry."

Here are some additional passages of scripture pertaining to the Bible.

Psalm 119:89 (NIV) says, "Your word, O LORD, is eternal; it stands firm in the heavens." The truth in God's Word never changes, and it will stand for eternity.

Joshua 1:8–9 (NIV) states:

> Do not let this Book of the Law depart from your mouth; meditate [implies a definite focusing of one's thoughts on something so as to understand it deeply] on it day and night, so that you may be careful to do everything written in it. Then you will be prosperous and successful. Have I not commanded you? Be strong and courageous. Do not be terrified; do not be discouraged; for the LORD your God will be with you wherever you go.

Look at how *Psalm 19:7–11 (NIV)* gives further guidance:

> The law of the LORD is perfect, reviving the soul. The statutes of the LORD are trustworthy, making wise the simple. The precepts of the LORD are right, giving joy to the heart. The commands of the LORD are radiant, giving light to the eyes. The fear of the LORD is pure, enduring forever. The ordinances of the LORD are sure and altogether righteous. They are more precious than gold, than much pure gold, they are sweeter than honey, than honey from the comb. By them is your servant warned; in keeping them there is great reward.

God loves us so much that He tells us in His Holy Bible how we can live an abundant life. This is how much God loves us. *Only God could give the gift of the Bible.*

Prayer

Have you ever thought about prayer and why it is an amazing gift from God and how prayer shows just how much God loves us?

As we consider this, *I think we need to look first at God and who He truly is in relation to man. We again need to realize God's total character. He is holy, righteous, just, and loving. God is God, and there is to be no other god before Him.* He is King of kings and Lord of lords. He is the Creator of the heavens and the earth and all that is within them. God is greater that any position of authority—any ruler, president, or person of royalty. He is the one and only Supreme Being. *Accordingly, we should never consider God with any attitude less than reverence, honor, and humility. Remember Malachi 1:11–14*, and we studied do not give God less than the best, or from *Proverbs 3:9–10* where we learned that we are not to give God less than the first fruits? Both of these passages of scripture apply when it comes to our prayer life as well.

Let us look at this a little deeper. From the Lord's Prayer *(Matthew 6:9–13 KJV)*, we are told in verse 9, "Our Father, who art in heaven, hallowed be thy name." *Hallowed* means holy. *God's name is holy, separate, and set apart from any other name.* God is called our Heavenly Father. To show how special God's name is, as our Heavenly Father, consider *Matthew 23:9 (KJV)*, which reads, "And call no man your father upon the earth; for one is your Father, who is in heaven."

Think about this. With all the other positions of authority stated above—rulers, presidents, royalty, CEOs of major corporations—how much access would you have to them? You would need clearance and a background check as well as an appointment. You would probably have just a certain amount of time with them. And more than likely a specific agenda that could be discussed.

I know of a CEO of a large corporation who is an extremely busy man. He has to restrict appointments and has a "No Solicitations" sign located at the entrance to his office. I am sure he constantly has request for donations, and I am convinced that he is a very generous man. My question is this—*is this man any busier than God, or does he have more request for assistance than God?*

Now contrast that with our Heavenly Father. *Hebrews 4:16 (KJV)* firmly stated, "Let us, therefore, come boldly unto the throne of grace, that we may obtain mercy, and find grace to help in time of need." *Do you find any conditions, such as would be necessary to approaching other dignitaries? Has God placed on us anything that must be done prior to our coming to Him in prayer? Has our Heavenly Father given us only a certain amount of time we can spend with Him in prayer? Do we need an appointment to come to God in prayer?* We can have access to God anytime, and we do not have to request prior permission to do so. Do you now see how truly special this gift of prayer is to the believer and how much God loves us and *yet keeping within His total character?*

Why did God give us this awesome privilege to boldly come to Him in prayer? What is His purpose in granting this gift to us? Here are some thoughts on the gift of prayer:

- It is through prayer that we develop a close relationship with God. *James 4:8 (NIV)* reads, "Come near to God and he will come near to you." Notice that action is upon us to draw near to God, then He draws near to us. *Drawing near to God is a choice. It is an individual decision and a commitment to do it.* We do this by spending time with God in prayer. *How do you get to know someone?* Spend time with them in deep conversation. *How can there actually be a close, personal relationship with God without prayer?* Prayer is vital for our spiritual growth and becoming a servant after God's own heart.

- It is through prayer that we can see God involved in our life. If you have not prayed about a matter when something does happen in your life, you will probably think of it as coincidence instead of God's provision. *But when you have prayed about something and it comes to pass, you know it is God answering your prayer, and He is the source. You see God working in your life through prayer.*

- Prayer releases God's power. *Jeremiah 33:3 (KJV)* tells us, "Call unto me, and I will answer thee, and show thee great and mighty things, which thou knowest not." God has the power to do things in our life beyond and greater than what we can imagine or envision. *Ephesians 3:20 (NIV)* says, "Now to him who is able to do immeasurably [we can't measure how great things God can do] more than all we ask or imagine, according to *his power* that is at work within us." *Read this again; is there anything more powerful than God? God's power works in each of us, individually and corporately.*

- Prayer aligns us with God's will for and in our lives. *Isn't this what we want and need, that God's will be done in our life?* Doesn't God alone know what is truly best for each of us individually?

- Prayer should be about God. It should serve His purposes before ours or that of humanity. *Accordingly, we should give God a reason He should answer our prayer. Have you ever thought about that, give God a reason to answer your prayer? Does it bring glory and honor to Him? Is it for His name's sake? Is it in accordance with God's will? Why should we give God a reason to answer our prayers? Does He not already know why He should or should not answer our prayers? Maybe it is for us to realize His purpose and His will in answering our prayers. That it does, in fact, bring glory to God or contribute to the growth of His kingdom. Giving God a reason to answer our prayers aligns us with God.*

- Prayer, Bible study, and the Holy Spirit all go together. We speak to God in prayer. He speaks to us through the Bible. God's will, will never be contrary to the Scriptures, *and the Holy Spirit's guidance will always align with the truth contained in the Bible.*

- Prayer should be given on the foundation of the sovereignty and total character of God. Accordingly, our prayers should be filled with praise, worship, adoration, supplication, confession, humility, and reverence.

- Prayer has power! *James 5:16 (NIV)* states, "The prayer of a righteous man is powerful and effective." Prayer has power and is effective.

- You are not alone in your praying. Jesus and the Holy Spirit are interceding for us to our Heavenly Father.

- Only God can answer prayer. He alone has the power, wisdom, and knowledge.

Someone once said that true prayer is God the Holy Spirit talking to God the Father, in the name of God, the Son Jesus, in the prayer room of the believer's heart. You may want to write this down.

Open this special gift from God daily. Savor and enjoy your time with Him. *Jeremiah 29:11–13 (NIV)* tells us, "For I know the plans I have for you, 'declares the LORD,' plans to prosper you and not to harm you, plans to give you hope and a future. Then you will call upon me and come and pray to me, and I will listen to you. You will seek me and find me when you seek me with all your heart." *Maybe this is the only condition God places on prayer—that we seek Him with all our heart.*

God has given us this gift of prayer because we are so important and special to Him, and only God could give us the gift of prayer. How can we not be in awe of Him?

Now I would like to briefly turn our attention to a few other things that only God can do.

Exodus 3:13–15 (KJV) states:

> And Moses said unto God, Behold, when I come unto the children of Israel, and shall say unto them, The God of your fathers hath sent me unto you; and they shall say to me, What is his name? What shall I say unto them? And God said unto Moses, I AM that I AM: and he said, thus shalt thou say unto the children of Israel, I AM hath sent me unto you.

Why did God identify himself as "I AM"? What is God saying to us when He says His name is "I AM"? If you think about this for a moment, you see God has revealed Himself as being who only God can be. What God said to Moses is that "I AM" all you will ever need, that is what "I AM." Anything in your life that you need, God is capable of taking care of for you. God says "I AM" anything and everything you will ever need.

Do you need love in your life? *First John 4:8 (KJV)* says, "God is love."

Do you need someone to care about you? "Casting all you care upon him; for he careth for you" *(1 Peter 5:7 KJV)*.

Do you need comfort? "I will not leave you comfortless; I will come to you" *(John 14:18 KJV)*.

Do you need peace in your life? "Peace I leave with you, my peace I give unto you; not as the world giveth, give I unto you. Let not your heart be troubled, neither let it be afraid" *(John 14:27 KJV)*.

Do you need joy? "And my soul shall be joyful in the LORD; it shall rejoice in his salvation" *(Psalm 35:9 KJV)*.

When God said, "I AM that I AM," what He is really saying is I AM all that you will ever need. "I am the way, the truth, and the life" *(John 14:6 NIV)*.

As we consider that God can supply all of our needs, it is important that we look deeper into this passage of scripture where God says, "I AM that I AM." There are certain areas of life in which God, and only God, is the true and ultimate source of our needs. In these situations, God alone can say, "I AM that I AM." Consider the following circumstances in which God alone can provide for us.

Only God can give us eternal life in heaven and that is through faith in His only begotten Son, Jesus Christ, as Lord and Savior. Not only is this what I firmly believe, but the Bible is very clear in stating that this is the only way to spend eternity with God in heaven. It is stated in John 14:6 and is further supported in Romans 10:9–10 and Acts 4:12. Man cannot obtain this through good deeds or living a good life in the eyes of his fellow man. It can only come from the grace of our loving and forgiving God and faith in His Son, Jesus Christ, as Lord and Savior.

Only God is the Creator of the heavens and the earth and all that is within them.

Only God can create life. In spite of the efforts of scientists, they cannot create life. Scientists may say they can create or clone life, but they are only using what God has permitted them to use.

Only God can truly and ultimately heal people of disease or save lives. I am amazed at what modern medicine can do and how it can improve our lives, but when God decides it is time for someone to leave this earth, it is going to happen, and there is nothing that will prevent it from taking place.

Only God can provide ultimate protection. He alone is our shield and defender. I am so very grateful for the personnel in our military, those in law enforcement, the firefighters, and the EMTs. I cannot express enough my gratitude and appreciation to the men and women who put their lives on the line daily for our protection and freedom. But they will be the first to state that they are not capable of protecting us the way God can and does.

Only God can give us eternal and everlasting peace. The Bible says there will be wars and talks of wars. It has happened virtually since the time of Adam and Eve. Nations fight against nations; neighbors fight and argue with each other; and brothers and sisters, parents and children, and husbands and wives all at one time or another have disputes with each other. But God alone has given us the Prince of Peace.

God alone can give us comfort. One of the roles of the Holy Spirit is to give comfort to God's children. We can get some comfort from family and friends or pastors and church family. However, when we experience the loss of a loved one or face a critical illness of a close family member, ultimately, comfort can only come from our Heavenly Father.

God, and no other, is able to say to us that I am the only source for eternal life in heaven. I am the only Creator. I am the only one that can create life. Only I am the Great Physician. I am the true source of your protection. I am the only one that can provide everlasting peace. And I am the only one that can give comfort and inner peace that is unexplainable in times of crisis.

There are certain things in life that God has reserved for Himself. He is a jealous God, and He will not share His glory with another. Accordingly, He alone is to be exalted with our praise and adoration. God alone is worthy to be honored and glorified.

Can we limit God's greatest blessings? I was sitting in a Sunday school class one Sunday morning, and the teacher was discussing the nation of Israel. He told us about how great the area of land of Israel was promised compared to what they actually possessed. According to Dr. David Jeremiah in his book *Is This The End?*, Israel was promised all of modern Israel, Lebanon, the West Bank of Jordan, and large parts of Syria, Iraq, and Saudi Arabia. Today, Israel is just a small strip of land on the Mediterranean coastline compared to the vast amount of land God had intended for them.

As I listened to our teacher, the thought came to me—*can we limit our blessings from God, and if so, why? Are we missing out of God's richest blessings because of something we do or don't do?*

Let me state here that we cannot limit God, but we can limit our benefits or blessings we receive from Him. As we look at the case of Israel, it was their disobedience that prevented them from possessing all the Promised Land God intended for them to receive.

A biblical example of this would be Adam. If you look at Genesis 3:22–24, we find that God banned him from the garden of Eden due to his disobedience. Can you imagine what Adam's life would have been like if he had never eaten from the tree of knowledge of good and evil? He missed out of God's riches blessings.

Another example is Moses (Numbers 20:1–13 and Deuteronomy 34:1–5). He was not allowed to enter the Promised Land because his actions did not show God's glory and power. He acted in anger and did not follow God's instructions as God told him.

Just as Adam, Moses, and the nation of Israel have not received God's greatest blessings because of their disobedience, we too miss out on them because of our disobedience. Look again at Jeremiah 33:3 and Ephesians 3:20, and think about what great and mighty things God could be doing in you and through you.

We have studied the four incredible gifts from God. Now I would like to look at God and His place in our lives and in society today.

This is my question. Have we lost a reverence or fear of God? Have we let society dilute our morals? Do we no longer stand in awe of God as God Almighty, the King of kings and Lord of lords? He is our God, our Creator, our Savior and Redeemer, our Teacher, Counselor, and Comforter. He is the Heavenly Father, our Lord and Savior, Jesus Christ, the Holy Spirit. All worthy of praise, honor, and glory.

So what does it mean to show reverence? Reverence is defined as deep respect, profound adoring, awed respect, awe, fear, and honor.

When Moses approached God in the burning bush, look at what God said to him in Exodus 3:5 (NIV): "Do not come any closer," God said, "Take off your sandals, for the place where you are standing is holy ground." This shows God demands and deserves our respect.

I believe that we have become too casual in our relationship with God, in our churches, our families, and in our daily walk with God. Do we truly stand in awe of Him? Do we show Him deep, profound, adoring respect and honor?

In David's writings, he states in *Psalm 89:5–7 (NIV):*

> The heavens praise your wonders, O LORD,
> your faithfulness too; in the assembly of the holy
> ones. For who in the skies above can compare
> with the LORD? Who is like the LORD among the
> heavenly beings? In the counsel of the holy ones
> God is greatly feared; he is more awesome than
> all who surround him. O LORD, God Almighty,
> who is like you? You are mighty, O LORD, and
> your faithfulness surrounds you.

If God is feared and reverenced like this in heaven, should we have any less respect for Him?

Let me challenge you to read Psalm chapter 86. Read it deeply and focus on what each verse is saying and then stand in awe and reverence of God, our Creator.

I am so thankful that God loves me and wants the best for me. I stand in awe of Him as God Almighty and Almighty God. *Psalms 86:12–13a (NIV)* says, "I will praise you, O Lord my God, with all my heart; I will glorify your name forever. For great is your love toward me."

The name of our God is worthy to be reverenced. May we stand in awe of Him!

With all that we see about how much God loves each of us, let us look at another psalm from David, king of Israel, about praise. Please read Psalm 145 in your Bible.

When you consider these four incredible gifts from God—Jesus, the Holy Spirit, the Holy Bible, and prayer and WHY He gave them—how can you not praise Him?

When you consider who God is and He still gave you these four incredible gifts, how can you not worship Him? He is the Creator. He IS the one true living God.

When you look at the love He has for you in giving these four incredible gifts, how can you not serve Him?

Praise God for what He has done and is doing.

Worship God for who He is. He IS God. The only true living God.

Serve God because you love Him.

Something important to consider: what would your life be like without these four incredible gifts from God? What would the world be like without each of them?

Marriage

Occasionally, I will get out my high school yearbooks and reminisce about classmates and events of that time in my life. Recently, I was looking at the pictures of my graduation class, and each member of the class listed their *ambition* by their picture. The majority of them, including myself, stated their ambition as living a happy, successful life. I believe this is a goal common to the majority of people—living a life that makes us feel fulfilled, meaningful, and worthwhile.

Earlier in our study, we looked at success. Now let us turn our attention to the pursuit of happiness.

Our Founding Fathers considered the pursuit of happiness a right when they wrote the Declaration of Independence: "We hold these truths to be self-evident, that all men are created equal, that they are endowed by their Creator with certain unalienable Rights, that among these are Life, Liberty, and the pursuit of Happiness." Although this right to happiness is not a guarantee, we do have the right to pursue happiness.

Exactly what are we looking for when we pursue happiness? Some thoughts are a sense that one's life has meaning and is worthwhile. It is a state of deep contentment and a positive state of well-being.

Happiness can be found in many different things and areas of life. What brings great joy and pleasure to one person may not bring happiness to another. I would like to concentrate on an area where most of us look for happiness—relationships. But I want to narrow this down even further to our family. And let us take it even deeper and look at our relationship with our spouse. There is no relationship that is more intimate than a husband and wife. *With this thought in mind, how can we make that relationship with our spouse stronger and become a source of deep happiness and contentment?*

There are many things in life whereby we work hard and put great effort in making it a success. Business owners and executives work long hours to have a successful business. Consider the time and effort athletic teams put in to have success on the playing field. People often spend large amounts of money and time on their hobbies and on recreational activities. All of these are worthwhile. *But do we put the same time and effort into bringing joy and happiness to our spouse? Since this is the most important relationship in our life, second only to our relationship with God our Creator, should we not put even greater effort into our marriage? Do we make an effort daily to make our spouse feel special?*

Think about this statement. Your spouse should be your greatest asset. In turn, you should be your spouse's greatest asset. If you want peace, harmony, and happiness in your life, will it not come from a loving, supportive relationship with your spouse? Are each of us doing things continually that build them up and not tear them down? If you make your spouse happy and content, does that not make you happy and content as well? This is where peace in your life will come from—a loving relationship where you work together *to have a happy, successful life.*

I know there are many of us that have great marriages. To have that, it takes work and effort. My parents celebrated their seventy-fifth anniversary a couple of years ago. It is a result of two loving people working together and being supportive of the other. They will tell you that one of the secrets to their successful marriage was a lot of giving on behalf of each of them.

Let me illustrate with a fable by Heather Forest and Susan Gaber about a contest between the sun and the wind and how it can relate to our happiness. One day, the sun and wind were having an argument as to which was stronger. They argued back and forth, with each presenting their case as to why they were stronger than the other. Finally, they decided to have a contest to settle the argument. There was a man walking down a country road. It was a nice day, but a little cool, so he had on a jacket. The sun and the wind determined that the one that could get the man to take off his jacket in the least amount of time would be the strongest.

The wind went first. Initially, the wind blew a gentle breeze. Then a little stronger, and a little stronger. But the harder the wind blew, the colder it got, and the more the man clenched his jacket around himself. He grabbed the top of his jacket with both hands to resist the force of the wind. Finally, the wind gave up.

Now it was the sun's turn. First, the sun started to gently warm the air. The man released his grip on his jacket. Then he unzipped it. As the sun continued to shine and warm the air, the man took off the jacket and continued his journey down the country road.

So what does this have to do with each of us in relation to our marriages? In relationships, we can be like the sun or the wind. We can argue and try to force our thoughts, opinions, beliefs, wants, and positions on the other person, and the result will be like the force of the wind. We will wrap ourselves tight and become more resistant. Or we can be like the sun and create an environment of warmth, concern, love, and caring. Note that both the wind and the sun used their greatest strength in the contest.

Which of the two, the sun or the wind, will result in a more peaceful, harmonious, happy marriage and home? And which will create resistance and less caring?

Look at Solomon's guidance from Proverbs, and please note that I believe these verses of scripture can apply to either the husband or the wife.

Proverbs 21:9 (NIV) says, "Better to live on a corner of the roof, than share a house with a quarrelsome wife." And from *Proverbs 21:19 (NIV):* "Better to live in a desert than with a quarrelsome and ill-tempered wife." Both of these verses would be the outcome from the wind in the story above. *Proverbs 17:1 (NIV)* states, "Better a dry crust with peace and quiet than a house full of feasting with strife."

So how are we going to become our spouse's greatest asset?

In my opinion, a woman's greatest need in a marriage is security, and a man's greatest need in a marriage is providing security. Do you agree or disagree with this statement?

Look at *Ephesians 5:22–33 (NIV)*, as I try to explain my thinking in this case:

> Wives, submit to your husbands as to the Lord. For the husband is the head of the wife as Christ is the head of the church, his body, of which he is the Savior. Now as the church submits to Christ, so also wives should submit to their husbands in everything. Husbands, love your wives, just as Christ loved the church and gave himself up for her to make her holy, cleansing her by the washing with water through the word, and to present her to himself as a radiant church, without stain or wrinkle or any other blemish, but holy and blameless. In this same way, husbands ought to love their wives as their own bodies. He who loves his wife loves himself. After all, no one ever hated his own body, but he feeds and cares for it, just as Christ does the church—for we are members of his body. For this reason a man will leave his father and mother and be united to his wife, and the two will become one flesh. This is a profound mystery—but I am talking about Christ and the church. However, each one of you also must love his wife as he loves himself, and the wife must respect her husband.

First, look at verse 31: "For this reason a man will leave his father and mother and be united to his wife, and the two will become one flesh." *What does it mean "and the two will become one flesh?"* I believe it is more than the intimate union between the husband and wife. I think it means they will be united in all things pertaining to the marriage and family. They are united, as stated in the verse, in raising the children, religion and spiritual matters, finances, political views, etc. There will be strife in the relationship if they are not unified in all things. *How can there be peace, harmony, and happiness in the marriage if they are not working together in all matters?*

Second, from verse 29: "No one ever hated his own body, but he feeds and cares for it." The updated NASB, as does the English Standard Version, says "nourishes and cherishes it."

What does it mean to nourish or nurture something? It means to feed or protect, to care for and encourage, contribute to the growth or development of someone or something, to provide for, cultivate, and to enlighten.

And what does it mean to cherish something? The meaning is to treasure, adore, hold in high esteem, to love, to protect and care for, to prize, and value.

Husbands, think about each of these definitions and how they apply to your wife and your responsibility as the spiritual leader in your home. You are to protect her, contribute to her spiritual growth, then adore, love, value, and treasure her.

Are not all of these providing for her security, as I stated earlier as being a woman's greatest need in marriage? And if the husband does these things, does that not appeal to his providing security, which I also stated previously? *In addition, if the man is doing all of these, is that not contributing to him becoming her greatest asset?* All of these are about providing some form of protection and security for the family. *And protection is more than keeping her from physical harm; it is protecting her spiritually, emotionally, mentally, and morally, as well as physically.*

One of the characteristics listed above that stands out to me is *treasure.* To treasure something is to have great value and appreciation of something, in this case our spouse. Think how the following verse of scripture applies in our marriage. *Matthew 6:21 (NIV) reads, "For where your treasure is, there your heart will be also."* Men, where is your heart? Where is your treasure? Are you constantly and continually doing those things that bring value to her life? This is all about being the spiritual leader in your home.

Now the question is how are you going to be the spiritual leader as we discussed? Let's return to *Ephesians 5:25–27 (NIV):* "Husbands, love your wives, just as Christ loved the church and gave himself up for her to make her holy, cleansing her by the washing with water through the word, and to present her to himself as a radiant church, without stain, wrinkle, or any other blemish, but holy and blameless."

Another question that goes along with this is how, as the spiritual leader of our wife, we can keep her radiant and without stain, wrinkle, or any other blemish, holy and blameless.

I believe the answer comes from what we studied in chapter 3 about guarding or protecting your (her) heart. *How do we guard or protect her heart?*

- Do your best to control (guard, protect) what her eyes see.
- Do your best to control (guard, protect) what her ears hear.
- Do your best to control (guard, protect) what goes into her mind.

Husbands, if we love her completely and nourish her through the Word of God, *will she not be holy, blameless, and radiant?* She will not be perfect, but she will be perfect for you.

Some time ago, I attended the funeral of a man I had known and respected since I was a child. I was visiting with his wife after the funeral and will never forget what she said about her husband: "He may not have been perfect, but he was perfect for me." There is something special about this relationship. They were married for over seventy years. This is what should be said about each of us by our spouse.

How can we have that in our marriage? This verse gives guidance for one way. *Daniel 1:8 (NIV) says,* "But Daniel resolved." Resolved means to do something, fixed in purpose or intent, strongly determined, fully committed.

Are you fully committed to your spouse for the long term—till death do you part? Will you do all you can to make your spouse your greatest asset, and will you do all you can to be your spouse's greatest asset?

I think it is interesting that the passage of scripture from Ephesians 5 (verses 22–24, 33) starts with the role of the wife and concludes with the duties of the wife.

In the context of these verses, what does it mean for the wife to submit to her husband? Basically, she is to submit and respect or honor her husband.

Submission, in my opinion, is not about dominance, being manipulated, or controlled by the husband. It is more about being protected and cared for, as the scripture states. They are one flesh and are to be united together for the good of the marriage and the family. It takes both the husband and wife, working together as a team and unified to have a successful marriage and relationship. Each fulfilling their respective roles to build up and not tear down what God has joined together. It is both of them submitting to God, as unto the Lord, according to the scripture, and making Him the head of their home, with the husband and wife both being like the sun and not the wind, as we discussed earlier in this chapter.

This is what *Proverbs 31:10–11, 28 (NIV)* says about a virtuous woman: "A wife of noble character who can find? She is worth far more than rubies. Her husband has full confidence in her, and lacks nothing of value. She brings him good, not harm, all the days of her life… Her children arise and call her blessed; her husband also, and he praises her." If you study *Proverbs 31*, I believe you will find a wife that is very much involved in every aspect of the family. She is active in doing multiple things that will build up and support her entire household, *she is priceless, and she has great value.*

I personally believe that if the husband takes his role seriously as the spiritual leader of the family that the wife will not have a problem or issue in submitting to his leadership. This is all within God's plan for the marriage.

Psalm 34:3 (NIV) says, "Glorify the LORD with me; let us exalt his name together." Can you see how this verse contributes to the husband and wife being one flesh if they glorify and exalt the Lord together?

Success is in the little things

Legendary coach John Wooden stated that success is in the details. It comes with taking care of the little things. To give you an example of how Coach Wooden practiced his belief in taking care of the small things, at the start of the very first practice of the season, he would personally show each player how to properly put on their socks. Then he would watch each player to be sure they understood the importance of this procedure. Why did he do this? Because wrinkles in socks caused blisters and blisters on the foot of his players meant they would not practice and play up to their greatest potential.

So what does knowing how to properly put on your socks have to do with marriage? One of the things necessary for a successful marriage is paying attention to the little things.

What are some recommendations that would lead to a more successful, blissful marriage? Here are some of my thoughts:

- Laugh together often. This may seem like an insignificant matter, but it really is important. *Proverbs 15:15 (NIV)* reads, "The cheerful heart has a continual feast."
- Talk to each other often. This is how you continue to grow in your relationship. It is also one of the comments wives state they need in their marriage.
- Husbands, ask your wife if she has money when she is leaving the house.
- Husbands, open the door for your wife and hold the chair for her when she is being seated. And wives, let your husband do this for you. This is a matter of respect and honor for each other.
- Make the time to be alone together.
- When you are walking past your spouse, kiss them on the cheek, forehead, or top of their head. Take the time to hold each other's hand. Make an effort to show each other special attention to make them feel how important they are to you.
- Share in the duties around the house and with taking care of the children. This is another area of comments made by wives that the husband does not share in helping with work at home.
- Be creative in ways to continually make your spouse feel special.

- Encourage and support each other to grow spiritually and in your daily walk with God. This would include prayer, Bible study, church, and spiritual training of the children.
- Always remember that you and your spouse are *one flesh*.

Coach Wooden is right; success is in taking care of the little things. Look at what Proverbs 1:32 (NIV) says and how it can apply to your marriage: "The complacency of fools will destroy them." Complacency in your marriage will destroy it. Pay close attention to the details.

Does following all the biblical principles stated in the Bible guarantee a successful marriage? No, they do not, because of the human element and factor involved. But the odds are greater for a successful marriage if you do follow these biblical principles.

Ecclesiastes 4:12 (b) (NIV) tells us, "A cord of three strands is not quickly broken." The cord of God, the husband, and the wife united and joined together as one cannot be quickly broken.

Some questions to consider pertaining to spiritual leadership and the family:

- *Is it easier for the man to grow spiritually if the wife is spiritual and continues to grow spiritually?*
- *Is it easier for the woman to grow spiritually if the man is spiritual and continues to grow spiritually?*
- *If one spouse is spiritual and the other is not, will there be peace and harmony or conflict in the marriage?*
- *How difficult would it be for the children to grow spiritually if their parents are not growing spiritually?*

Remember this thought pertaining to marriage—the greater the commitment, the greater the reward.

Children and Grandchildren

"Train up a child in the way he should go and, when he is old, he will not depart from it" *(Proverbs 22:6 KJV)*.

In the context of our study about becoming a servant after God's own heart, what is the meaning of this verse?

First, I believe it is a general statement that *if* a child is properly trained, they will retain that training when they become an adult.

Second, it is instruction that we should properly train children, so they will conduct themselves properly when they become an adult.

Throughout my life, when I have read this verse of scripture, I have thought of the giving of religious or spiritual training to children—and when they are adults. Even though they may backslide at times, they will go back to their religious teaching. This is true of this verse, but I think there is more to it. This verse can apply to any type of training we give our children, whether spiritual, moral, social, educational, or financial. The key word from the verse above is *train*. In this case, it means to discipline, to instruct, and to educate. It is also a military term. When soldiers go off to boot camp, the purpose is to teach them how to succeed and survive in battle. They are trained to protect themselves and their fellow soldiers and how to avoid danger.

Our children are in a battle, and the battle intensifies when they become adults. Just as a soldier should not be sent into battle unprepared, we should not send our children out into the adult world without proper training and preparation. Considering that the pre-adult life is eighteen to twenty years long and adult life may span more than fifty years, we must teach our children how to live successfully as adults because the majority of their lives will be lived as an adult. Why would we send our children out into an adult world without proper training and preparation? This is the parent's responsibility and a part of the role as a spiritual leader of the family. We are to prepare their hearts for the fight they will be facing

What are some of the tools Satan uses to capture the hearts, minds, and souls of young people and even adults today?

- Advertising
- Television
- Music
- Video games
- News media
- Social media
- Art
- Various forms of print—books, magazines, etc.
- Politicians or political ideology
- Judicial system
- Educational system
- Acceptance

I want to expand on the acceptance as being one of Satan's tools to gain control of our young people. What I am referencing here is that we must accept others regardless of their practice of alternative lifestyles or gender identity.

Many of the things the Bible calls sin is now being promoted and even glamorized, and those who believe it is sin are called a bigot. It has even gotten to the point where some people are misquoting scripture from the Bible to support their views instead of searching the Bible for God's truth. This is all part of the lies and deception of the enemy.

Where do we start in the training of our children?

Proverbs 13:22 (NIV) states, "A good man leaves an inheritance for his children's children."

I want to change this to state, "A good man leaves a LEGACY for his children's children."

As the spiritual leader of your family, what kind of legacy will you leave?

What is the difference between a legacy and an inheritance? Actually, they are very similar in meaning. An inheritance deals more with the passing down of assets or physical traits while legacy deals more with character and reputation. I believe this verse of scripture could apply to either definition. In *Leadership Promises for Your Week,* John Maxwell (Thomas Nelson, Inc. 2007) states, "An inheritance is something you leave *to* someone. But a legacy you leave is something you leave *in* someone" (emphasis mine). *What are you leaving in your family or the people that you come in contact with throughout your life?*

As parents and grandparents, God has given us a tremendous responsibility. Our children and grandchildren are ours as gifts from God, and He has placed us in a position of trusteeship or stewardship over them. A trustee is a person who holds and manages property for another. In this case, we are trustees over God's child, His creation. A steward is a person in charge of another's business. We are God's trustees or stewards, and He expects us to be good soil in which our children are planted. *First Corinthians 4:2 (KJV)* reads, "Moreover, it is required in stewards, that a man be found faithful." And from *2 Timothy 1:14 (NASB),* "Guard, through the Holy Spirit who dwells in us, the treasure which has been entrusted to you." We are to be good stewards and to guard or protect those treasures (children and grandchildren) God has entrusted to our care.

Look at God's instruction to us from *Deuteronomy 32:46 (NIV)*: "Take to heart all the words I have solemnly declared to you this day, so that you may command your children to obey careful all the words of this law. They are not just idle words for you—*they are your life.*" God instructs us in His Word, the Holy Bible, how to raise our children and His instructions are *"they are your life."*

Something we discussed earlier in this study, but it certainly applies here, is concerning the Ten Commandments. The first four commands are about our relationship to God. The fifth is we are to honor our father and mother, and the remaining five are about our relationship with our fellow man. What is interesting to me is the location of honoring our parents. Could that be because the parents are the anchor or bridge to connect God with the children? And that the parents are to train up the children to honor and reverence God first and then train them in their relationship with others, considering that the family is the most basic unit in society?

In conversation with many parents, with adult children, they share a common problem they are facing. They raised their children in church, and many of their children have made a profession of faith in Jesus as Lord and Savior. After their kids left home, they no longer attend church, and their lives are not bearing any notable spiritual fruit, so to speak. They have taken on the world's teachings, which are all a part of Satan's lies and deception. Some are even questioning their salvation and God's teaching.

I wish I had an answer to this problem, but here is one thing I know. We, as a society, are reaping what we have sown. *Galatians 6:7–8 (NIV)* firmly states, "Do not be deceived; God cannot be mocked. A man reaps what he sows. The one who sows to please his sinful nature, from that nature will reap destruction; the one who sows to please the Spirit, from the Spirit will reap eternal life." Again, as a society we are reaping what we have sown, and we are being deceived by Satan and the world.

Now look at our instruction from *Galatians 6:9 (NIV):* "Let us not become weary in doing good, for at the proper time we will reap a harvest if we do not give up." We are not to give up on teaching and training our children, even after they become an adult. We need to stand firm in our pursuit of becoming a servant after God's own heart as we lead our children and grandchildren. This is a need which will require a lot of prayer for guidance and wisdom from God.

Where do we start in our efforts to be the spiritual leader for our children? There are two passages of scripture that give us guidance.

First comes from *Ephesians 6:4 (NIV):* "Fathers, do not exasperate your children; instead, bring them up in the training and instruction of the Lord." The KJV states to "bring them up in the nurture and admonition of the Lord." This is an awesome responsibility, but it is vital for the spiritual growth of the children to bring them up in the training and instruction of the Lord. Church and Sunday school are there to support and add to what the parents are doing at home, not to take the place of home instruction and training.

A personal thought is that we should have our young children reading and studying the Bible themselves as soon as they are mentally ready to do so. This teaches them a love and appreciation for the Word of God. As parents, we should give instruction and training for their *understanding* of what the truth is in the Scriptures. *Psalm 119:9 (NIV)* reads, "How can a young man keep his way pure? By living according to your word."

The second passage which I believe gives full support to the verse from Ephesians 6 is *Deuteronomy 11:18–20 (NIV)*:

> Fix these words of mine in your hearts and minds; tie them as symbols on your hands and bind them on your foreheads. Teach them to your children, talking about them when you sit at home and when you walk along the road, when you lie down and when you get up. Write them on the doorframes of your houses and, on your gates,…

From these verses, is there ever a time when we are not to teach God's Word to our children? We are to do it at home, when walking or traveling, at bedtime, and when we get up in the morning; morning and night we are to be nurturing and admonishing our children in how they should walk with the Lord. We are to continually fill the hearts and minds of our children and grandchildren with the Word and teachings of God because that is what Satan and the world are doing, continually filling their minds with things of the world. This is your responsibility as the spiritual leader in the home.

So this is my recommendation for young parents and what they could do to prevent their children from leaving their faith and spiritual training when they become adults. I believe if you would start having your children read the Bible at the youngest age possible, they can get the Word of God inside them. Remember back to Session 4 when we discussed all the food in a grocery store does you no good until you eat it and get it inside you. We also discussed that to learn how to play a musical instrument, the individual must take lessons, study, and practice the instrument themselves. Perhaps reading the Bible at an early age will develop a love for God's Word and carry on with them through their lives. This practice should be done as long as they live in your household. It would be even better if the parents asked biblical questions relating to what their children are reading to encourage them to think, consider, and hopefully *understand* what God is trying to teach them. This would require spiritual maturity on the part of the parent, but this would further help the parents in the path to spiritual growth. It is vital that they get the Word of God inside them so that they will know God's truth and not be deceived by Satan and the teachings of the world.

What are some of the values, as the spiritual leader, we should teach and instill in our children and grandchildren, so they will become servants after God's own heart? The values they will learn in and through us? Where do we begin?

Guard their heart

This is something we have previously looked at in this study, but I believe it is important to repeat it in this session about training our children and grandchildren. *Proverbs 4:23 (NIV) says, "Above all else, guard your heart, for it is the wellspring of life."* Above all else, guard and protect your and their heart. The New Living Translation reads, "Guard your heart above all else, for it determines the course of your life." *Above all else—what does this mean?* Protecting your heart is to be your top priority. To guard it would be like posting guards around a military camp to keep the enemy from sneaking up on you. Protect your heart by being alert to those things that could damage or destroy your heart. A wellspring is the place where something comes from or starts. Protect your heart because the heart is where the issues, morals, and character of your life begin.

As their spiritual leader, we should do the following:

- We are to control, guard, and protect what their eyes see.
- We are to control, guard, and protect what their ears hear.
- We are to control, guard, and protect what goes into their mind.
- We are to control, guard, and protect their heart.
- We are to control, guard, and protect who becomes their friends and companions. *Proverbs 13:20 (NIV) tells us,* "He who walks with the wise grows wise, but a companion of fools suffers harm." *First Corinthians 15:33 (NIV) says,* "Do not be misled; 'Bad company corrupts good character.'" *This caution applies to adults as well as young people.*

What is the best way to guard and protect your heart? Spending time to *study, learn, and apply* the Word of God. *Psalm 119:105 (NIV) says, "Your word is a lamp to my feet and a light for my path." What does this verse mean?* The Bible gives us guidance and direction in how we should live our lives. *Here is a* thought question *for you. Is there anything in the Bible that is bad for you? Does it not actually enhance your life?*

Going back to Proverbs 22:9 about training up a child, what are some character traits we should be teaching, training, and being an example for our children and grandchildren?

Your name is not for sale

Proverbs 22:1 (KJV) says, "A good name is rather to be chosen than great" riches, and loving favor rather than silver and gold."

I want to share with you a biblical example of what it means to value your good name. Let us look at the life of Job. Job had everything—wealth, family, prestige, good health, and friends. One day, a servant came with the news that all of his possessions had been destroyed. Another servant came in with the news that all of his children had been killed. Then, Job's health turned bad, and he had painful sores all over his body.

Job's friends accused him of committing some great sin that had caused all of the problems. His wife even told him to curse God and die. Job could have given up, but he knew what was worth fighting for. Notice how Job responded to his accusers in *Job 27:3–6 (KJV):*

> *All the while my breath is in me and the spirit of God is in my nostrils; My lips shall not speak wickedness, nor my tongue utter deceit. God forbid that I should justify you; till I die I will not remove mine integrity from me. My righteousness I hold fast, and will not let it go; my heart shall not reproach me as long as I live.*

Job knew he had not done anything to cause the hardships that had happened to him. But look again at his reaction. *Notice his intensity and most of all his integrity.*

"Till I die I will not remove mine integrity from me." He would not let anything take away his integrity.

"My righteousness I hold fast, and will not let it go." He guarded and clung to his righteousness because it was precious, valuable, and priceless to him.

"My heart shall not reproach me as long as I live." This was a lifetime commitment for Job. He would not do anything that might harm or damage his good name. Job was protecting his heart, his righteousness, and his integrity.

Look at what *Proverbs 3:3–4 (NIV) says about the value of a good name: "Let love and faithfulness never leave you, bind them around your neck, write them on the table of your heart. Then you will win favor and a good name in the sight of God and man." Herein lies the key to a good name—love and faithfulness.* Notice that our good name comes *after* we show love and faithfulness, not before, and they are to never leave us.

Love is defined as strong affection and concern for another person, brotherly loyalty, benevolent concern, and worshipful adoration. *Love is an extremely powerful character trait when put into practice.*

Faithfulness is defined as steadfast in affection, loyalty, firm in adherence to promises or duty, and adhering to or firmly devoted to someone or something. *Are these not characteristics you want to see in yourself, as well as others, especially family members?*

Looking back at verses 3 and 4, we are told to "bind them around your neck and write them on the table of your heart." The neck is the base of the head, indicating binding them in your mind so that you will be continually thinking about acting in love and faithfulness. The heart, again, is where the issues of life begin.

So what is your name worth? When you are on the side of what is morally right (and there is a big difference between what is morally right and legally right), you are never wrong, and you will not need to worry about your decisions or conduct. You will not need to worry about trying to keep something covered up or from being revealed. The result is less tension and greater peace of mind, and love and faithfulness will help build your legacy.

What to leave behind

Philippians 4:8 (KJV) says, "Finally, brethren, whatever things are true, whatever things are honest, whatever things are just, whatever things are pure, whatever things are lovely, whatever things are of good report: if there be any virtue, and if there be any praise, think on these things."

Are the character qualities listed here not how you want to be remembered and are vital to leaving our spiritual legacy in and to our children and grandchildren? Look again at the characteristics listed in this scripture: true, honest, just, pure, lovely, and admirable or a good report. We are to be truthful or trustworthy; honest and righteous; have purity of thought, speech, and deeds; be loving; and conduct ourselves so that good things are said about us. *Are these not character qualities of life that you want to teach your children and grandchildren? Are these not the qualities that you want them to see in you?*

Let's look at each of these character qualities:

- Whatever things are true—this would be to avoid being deceptive, false, and to be truthful in all things. *Think about this. If you cannot trust someone ALL the time, then you cannot trust them any time because you will never know when the time will be that they fail your trust.*

- Whatever things are honest—this would be honesty, integrity, respect, and reverence.

- Whatever things are just—we are to be guided by truth, righteousness, fairness, and justice. Doing what is right and acceptable according to moral principles. It would be obedience to God's Laws as well as civil laws when they do not conflict with the Laws of God.

- Whatever things are pure—this would be striving to live a holy life, with clean thoughts, deeds, actions, and words.

- Whatever things are lovely would be showing love and living a life worthy of love. Think about what actions show love to others, especially to your spouse, children, and grandchildren.

- Whatever things are of good report—this would be living a life that is gracious, well-spoken of, and admirable. Doing those things in which other people will give a good report about you.

- If there be any virtue—virtue is defined as moral excellence, righteous, of good moral character. *Proverbs 31:10 (KJV) states, "Who can find a virtuous woman? For her price is far above rubies."* A virtuous person, woman or man, is priceless.

- If there be any praise—we are not to seek the praise of men, but we are to live our lives in a manner worthy of praise. We should live our lives so that if any one says anything bad about us, no one will believe them. *Remember this—one bad action can ruin a lifetime of good. A biblical example of this would be King David. When you first hear King David mentioned, you immediately think about David and Goliath or David and Bathsheba. Consider this—would you think more highly of King David if he had never had the relationship with Bathsheba?*

As verse 8 is concluded, look at what we are to do: "Think [meditate] on these things." Meditate means intense thinking to a point where your thoughts become a way of life. We are to concentrate our thinking on the characteristics listed in this passage.

As we are teaching our children and grandchildren a moral lifestyle, the next verse from *Philippians 4:9 (KJV) places much responsibility on us as parents and grandparents: "Those things which ye have both learned, and received, and heard, and seen in me, do, and the God of peace shall be with you."*

Those things *learned* are what we have taught them. Those things *received* are the gifts, including values of a spiritual nature, we give to them. I would also include the gift of our name and the value of a good name as we discussed earlier. Those things *heard* are the things that we have said to them and the things others say about us, good or bad. Those things *seen* are what they see us do.

What example are you setting for your children and grandchildren? Are you proud of the things they have learned, received, heard, and seen in you?

Now consider the promise God gives us when we live morally responsible lives according to His will and as stated in this passage. Look again at *Philippians 4:9: "And the God of peace shall be with you."* Your life and the lives of your family will be lived in peace, and the God of peace will be with you when you live your life within His will. *Think about this. Do you have peace in your life when your children are continually disobedient and disrespectful?* Peace comes from obedience to God's instructions both in our lives and in the lives of our children and grandchildren.

Philippians 4:7 tells us, "And the peace of God, which passeth all understanding, shall keep your hearts and minds through Christ Jesus."

Your spiritual legacy

I would like to take you into the future and assume you are attending your own funeral. You are there in spirit, and no one knows you are there.

Imagine, if you will, what it will be like. What do you want said about you? How do you want to be eulogized? Do you want to be remembered as a good spouse and parent, a good provider for your family, and a generous and caring person? Will the speaker's job be easy or difficult to say nice and comforting words about you? If he does say nice things about you, will those in attendance believe him? Will he say your integrity was without question and that you loved the Lord and served Him faithfully?

I feel that this is how everyone wants to be remembered—not as mean, selfish, uncaring, or dishonest. *The way you want to be remembered after you are gone is how you should live your life while you are on this earth. This sets your goals for your life. Look again at Philippians 4:8 (KJV): "Finally, brethren, whatever things are true, whatever things are honest, whatever things are just, whatever things are pure, whatever things are lovely, whatever things are of good report: if there be any virtue, and if there be any praise, think on these things."*

Are the character issues listed here not how you want to be remembered and leave as our spiritual legacy? Look again at the characteristics listed in this scripture: true, honest or noble, just, pure, lovely, and admirable or things of a good report. We are to be truthful and trustworthy; honest and righteous; have purity of thought, speech, and deeds; be loving; and conduct ourselves so that good things are said about us.

When you go to be with the Lord and your family is going through your possessions, what will they find from your books, magazines, receipts, and bank statements? Think about this—your bank statement and canceled checks *reveal you* and will show your true character. Will they not show where your heart was? Will your family find a life of godliness or worldliness? When they go through your Bible, will they find it marked and worn from use, or will they find it unused and covered with dust?

A final verse of scripture about leaving our legacy is in Proverbs 29:7 (NKJV): "The righteous man walks in his integrity; His children are blessed after him."

This is your spiritual legacy, what you leave behind. It shows if you have a heart after God's own heart.

The Dignity of Work

You are scheduled to interview for a job that you really want. A final review of your resume is complete, just to be sure everything is up to date and accurate. You make sure you look your best. While driving to the interview, you rehearse the things you are going to say and questions you want to ask. Earlier this morning, you read in the Bible where you are to have a humble spirit. So you have a problem. How can you be humble yet tell your potential employer how great you are and that you are the best candidate for the position with his or her company? *Does the scripture not apply in this case? What would God want you to do?*

Does God want you to be a success? And in the context of this portion of our study in becoming a servant after God's own heart, how does God want us to conduct ourselves in the workplace?

What is success in the eyes of God? I think, first, we need to determine what success is and what is failure. Success to me, as I stated earlier in our study, is becoming the person God wants us to be and being obedient to His will in our life, and accordingly, being blessed by God for our being faithful. It is being a good steward with the time, talents, gifts, and opportunities He gives us. Failure would be just the opposite or not becoming the person God wants us to be and not being obedient to His will.

Why would God want us to succeed? "So whether you eat or drink or whatever you do, do it all for the glory of God" *(1 Corinthians*

10:31 NIV). All that we do is to be done to bring glory to God, not to us individually. *Does this not go along with my definition of success that I stated above?*

The question now becomes how are we to glorify God in our work?

A topic of several conversations I have had recently concern the work ethic of today's workforce. I know that there are many people, of all ages, that are very good workers and a great asset to their employers. But that is not always the case. In fact, there are many people today that would criticize a person that works hard. Even our politicians pass laws that encourage not working as opposed to laws that reward working and becoming a success.

Have you ever thought about how your work ethic reflects on your reputation, character, and your Christian witness? The work environment and your public life is probably where you are most watched and for others to see "your life and your integrity." They see how you react in certain situations and if are you consistent in your spiritual walk with God. Your pursuit of a heart like God's is on public display in the workplace and public squares.

My wife and I have ten grandchildren. When each of the oldest four reached the age of sixteen, I had a one-on-one talk with them about the dignity of work. I hope to be able to continue this when the other six reach the age of sixteen.

The basic topic of the conversation with these four grandchildren was *"Regardless of who signs your paycheck, you really, in fact, work for yourself."* I explained that a poor work ethic was a reflection on them and their character and that they would be paid and promoted accordingly. A good work ethic would result in more pay and promotions. If not from their current employer, then another employer would see or hear about them, but eventually, their success in work would depend on having a good work ethic.

To support this, consider that the other employees of the company talk and discuss those that are slack in their work. These comments are made not only at work among coworkers but also out in the public with their friends and families. Also, the supervisor knows those staff members on which they can depend and those they cannot. *Which has the greatest potential for success—a good work ethic or a poor one?*

In a recent conversation with a close friend, we were discussing the problem many employers are having today finding good employees. During the conversation, he mentioned an acquaintance of his that worked for his dad. My friend stated that this man, probably in his thirties, slept late and showed up for work around midmorning. I am sharing this conversation to illustrate the point that people talk about those with a poor work ethic. Are there any of you that own a business or those of you in a management position that would hire this individual for your company?

Consider also about how a poor work ethic affects your Christian witness. Will someone be more likely to listen to the gospel from a person with a good work ethic compared to one with a poor work ethic? Look at what *Colossians 3:23 (NIV)* says: "Whatever you do, work at it with all your heart, as working for the Lord, not for men." We are to work with all our heart as if working for the Lord. One reason for this is our Christian witness. We read further in *Proverbs 18:9 (NIV):* "One who is slack in his work is a brother to one who destroys." *What does being slack in your work destroy?* It destroys time, revenue, reputation (both the employee and the employer), character, training, and your Christian witness. Think how others are affected when someone is slack in their work; they have to work harder. *And what does being slack in work build up?* Nothing at all comes to my mind.

This is not to say that the employer has no responsibility for the success of the employee. They should provide a good work environment and pay a fair wage according to the job skills and education required, local salary structure, and economic environment. They should have clear, concise policies stating what is expected of the entire staff, and they should provide proper, ongoing training and supervision to ensure the success of the employee and the company. In addition, they should recognize and reward those that contribute to the success of the company.

Work is honorable, and we need to educate our children, and in some cases adults, to this fact. There should be dignity in work. Dignity means worthy of honor and respect. In this case, worthy of dignity to ourselves, our employer, and our Heavenly Father. I personally believe the crime rate among youth would drop dramatically if we put these young people to work. When they have unproductive time on their hands and they are constantly hanging out with their peers is when trouble breeds. In my opinion, one of the greatest failures of the US Congress was when they passed the law that a company could not hire a person under the age of sixteen. Our youth are missing numerous life lessons by not learning good work and life skills during the informative, learning years of their life. This is when they should learn the dignity of work.

As a sidenote to my comments about our youth, I would love to see after-school programs that teach and encourage work. There are a lot of great programs and organizations, such as the Boys Club, YMCA, YWCA, and others sponsored by well-known athletes, but most of these are about sports and athletics. *What about an after-school program teaching work skills and work ethic?* These young people could actually do jobs for pay, such as washing police cars, school buses, ambulances, fire trucks, etc. They could clean up parks and roadways and assist the janitorial staff at school. In addition, one or two afternoons a week could be dedicated to classroom teaching about work skills, how to interview for a job, what would be expected on a job, and how to dress for a job. The programs could be funded through grants, sponsorships, and even taxes, possibly through savings from reduced crime. Perhaps the local chamber of commerce, churches, and possibly the small business administration could be involved to provide their expertise to the project. I would suggest that there could be volunteers that would be more than happy to share their time and experiences with these young people and to have a positive impact on the future of our country.

People should be educated and encouraged to grow and develop. To grow is to develop naturally, to become better by degrees, and to mature. Develop is to improve or build up and progress.

Is life not about growth and development? Do we not progress in our education? Does a sport team not practice to improve? Why should our career and work be any different? We should not be content to get the *minimum* out of life, including our work. *First*

Corinthians 9:24 (KJV) says, "Know ye not that they who run in a race run all, but one receiveth the prize? So run, that ye may obtain." We are to strive to obtain the prize, not to be satisfied with the *minimum.*

I believe in a system that builds up our fellow man and not in one that tears down. What is wrong with a system that encourages success, growth and accomplishment, and individual effort, so we can contribute to the benefit of others and for the betterment of society? To me, that is where our true reward is found.

God has a purpose in everything He does. *With that thought in mind, why did God decree or ordain that men and women should work?*

I personally believe that God wants us to live productive, useful lives. Throughout the Bible, we are instructed in scripture to build up others and to be a servant. *When we do positive things for others, do we not also receive a blessing? Proverbs 11:25 (NIV)* states, "A generous man will prosper; he who refreshes others will himself be refreshed." Since we are currently studying the dignity of work, I would like to look at this verse in the context of work. Taking this verse and stating "he who is productive will himself be refreshed," the person who is doing positive things will be happy and refreshed. *What is the opposite of happy? Is it not being sad and depressed? Is depression not a major issue people face today?*

I have a nephew that is a physician's assistant, who works in the emergency room of a major hospital. I was discussing his work with him one day, and he talked about a patient he was treating for depression. He asked the patient what he did for a living. The reply was that he was on welfare and did not work. My nephew replied that, that was why he was depressed—because he needed to feel he was doing something positive in his life. We need to be doing things continually that bring personal fulfillment in our life, and the workplace is one of those areas in which we can find personal satisfaction and reward and that we are making a positive difference.

Let us look at a couple of passages of scripture that I believe support my belief. *Ecclesiastes 2:24–25 (NIV)* says, "A man can do nothing better than to eat and drink and find satisfaction in his work.

This too, I see, is from the hand of God, for without him, who can eat or find enjoyment?" Then from *Ecclesiastes 5:18–20 (NIV):*

> Then I realized that it is good and proper for a man to eat and drink, and to find satisfaction in his toilsome labor under the sun during the few days of life God has given him—for this is his lot. Moreover, when God gives any man wealth and possessions, and enables him to enjoy them, to accept his lot and be happy in his work—this is a gift of God. He seldom reflects on the days of his life, because God keeps him occupied with gladness of heart.

God knew, in His wisdom, that man needs to be productive, and when he is doing positive things in his work, he will find joy and happiness.

Another thing to also consider is, in my personal opinion, *the workplace or business environment is where we are most exposed to temptation and compromise godly principles.* Improper comments, conduct, or advances that could lead to inappropriate relationships. Others are tempted to look for ways not to report all the income on taxes. Employees abuse supplies, telephone, and even time doing personal business while on the company time clock. It has become the way of life in corporate America.

Something also of major importance is that the workplace, with the exception of our family and church, is the place where we can have the greatest spiritual impact through how we conduct our everyday life at work. People see how you react in all situations to see if you are consistent in your spiritual walk.

There is a biblical example that I think gives us guidance concerning the heart of a servant after God's own heart in the workplace and utilizing the time, talents, gifts, abilities, and opportunities God gives us. It comes from *Matthew 25:14–30* where Jesus tells the parable of the talents. And I want to emphasize that this is Jesus's teachings. If you will recall, the lord was going on a journey to a foreign country. Before he left, he delivered to his servants his goods for them to oversee while he was gone. To one servant he gave five talents, another two talents, and a third servant he gave one talent. To each servant he gave goods according to their ability.

The servant with five talents traded the goods and made another five talents. The servant with two talents traded and made another two talents. But the servant with one talent hid the talent in the ground. When the lord returned and inquired about his goods, notice that he praised the good and faithful servants and increased their responsibilities. He rewarded them for being good stewards with the goods he had placed in their care. He further told them to enter into the joy of their lord. But when the servant with one talent returned the goods to the lord, the lord was angry and condemned the unfaithful servant for not being a good steward. Then the lord punished the unfaithful servant.

Further, verse 28 tells us that the lord took the talent from the unfaithful servant and gave it to the one who originally had five talents. *Why would the lord do this?* Verse 29 gives us the answer: "For everyone who has will be given more, and he will have an abundance. Whoever does not have, even what he has will be taken from him" (NIV). God rewards those that are faithful with the gifts and talents He gives them. He wants us to be good stewards and to add to the value or expand what He has entrusted unto us to oversee for Him. *First Timothy 6:20* tells us to guard what has been entrusted to our care. We could substitute our name for Timothy when reading this verse of scripture. Good stewardship is rewarded while being unfaithful is punished. *Why would we expect God to reward us with more when we are not faithful with what He has already given us?* If we are good stewards, we will be given more and we will have abundance. Why? Because God knows we will take good care of His possessions. Good stewardship, in a little, leads to being entrusted with more. God rewards faithfulness with new opportunities and responsibilities.

Assume you are the owner, CEO, or manager of a business. What are some of the principles, qualities, characteristics, or the foundation of a good work ethic that you would look for in your staff members or that you as a leader should possess? Here are a few of my thoughts:

- Be punctual. Always be on time, whether it is reporting for work at the beginning of your work period or coming back from lunch.

- Do more than the job description requires. Minimum work gets minimum pay. Your employer will appreciate this, and you will learn more. Remember that with wisdom and knowledge, there is power.

- Communicate with your boss or supervisor, but do not complain. Communicate for the success of the company.

- Take care of the little details. I love to read about John Wooden, perhaps the greatest basketball coach of all time. Coach Wooden said, "Big things are accomplished only through the perfection of minor details." There is a lot of *business wisdom* in this statement. Waste, uncontrolled expenses or debt, untrained or poorly trained staff—all can quickly destroy a company. At least, the company will not produce at maximum performance. In sports, a coach will train an athlete to use the proper technique, so they can play to a high level each and every game. They teach them the little things, so they can do great things. Look at what Proverbs says about waste. *Proverbs 18:9 (KJV) says, "He also who is slothful in his work is brother to him that is a great waster." Proverbs 10:4 (KJV) tells us, "He becometh poor that dealeth with a slack hand but the hand of the diligent maketh rich."* In business and athletics, there is no such thing as a small mistake.

- You gain a tremendous advantage when you are well trained and better educated. *I love this statement—you will never go broke investing in yourself.* Training and education are investments in yourself. *Proverbs 22:3–4 (NIV)* states, "By wisdom a house is built and through understanding it is established; through knowledge its rooms are filled with rare and beautiful treasures." Think how this verse applies to you. Now substitute your occupation or business for house in the verse above and read it again.

- A good work ethic helps overcome depression. We can easily become depressed when there are no positive things happening in our lives. If, in our work, we see progress being made, goals achieved, and there is a feeling of contribution, we have a better personal attitude. It contributes to a better state of mind when we feel we are making a difference; that something is better because we are a part of it.

- Dress appropriately for the job and position you currently have and for the image the job should portray. Sometimes the current fashion trends are inappropriate, and be sure to get your employer's approval prior to wearing anything of a political nature. Use good judgment in these matters. Make your overall appearance a priority.

- Your name is not for sale. Please remember that your name represents you, your employer, your family, and Christ. Be a person of good character, honesty, and integrity. Always use good manners, and be respectful of others. *Proverbs 22:1 (NIV)* says, "A good name is more desirable than great riches; to be esteemed is better than silver or gold." Look again at *Philippians 4:8–9 (KJV):* "Finally, brethren, whatever things are true, whatever things are honest, whatever things are just whatever things are pure, whatever things are lovely, whatever things are of good report; if there be any virtue, and if there be any praise, think on these things. Those things which ye have both learned, and receive, and heard and seen in me, do, and the God of peace shall be with you." *Are these not character qualities we need to display in the workplace and that we would want in every member of our staff?*

- Be very careful and cautious of what you say. Guard your mouth. Be quick to praise others and slow to criticize them. Avoid being a gossip and never use profanity. We are to be good stewards of our tongue. This is a part of our Christian witness. It reflects on your character and your reputation.

Proverbs 4:24 (NIV) reads, "Put away perversity from your mouth; keep corrupt talk far from your lips."

- What you do on your personal time away from work still reflects on your employer. *It also shows your true character.*
- I personally believe that everything in which you are involved should be better because you are a part of it. *Are you making a positive contribution? Would you be missed if you were no longer associated?*
- Since our study is about becoming a servant after God's own heart, there are two other *biblical* character qualities I believe we should have as God's witness and representative in a work environment and in all other areas of our life as well. I also believe that these two characteristics work together and build up each other. Those two character traits are humility and having a servant's heart. The opposite of humility is pride. Pride is being and caring about yourself, whereas humility is about others and bringing glory to God, as we are instructed in scripture to do. Also, we are told to strive to be like Jesus, the ultimate example of a servant who put others before themself. Both of these characteristics show we are striving to become a servant after God's own heart. Two passages of scripture from the undated New American Standard Bible that I believe support this are *Proverbs 22:4:* "The reward of humility and fear of the LORD are riches, honor and life" and from *Matthew 23:11–12:* "But the greatest among you shall be your servant. Whoever exalts himself shall be humbled; and whoever humbles himself shall be exalted." Please consider how both of these passages would apply in the workplace.

We are told to emulate Jesus in our actions. Look at what Jesus says in *John 5:17 (NIV):* "Jesus said to them, 'My Father is always at his work to this very day, and I, too, am working.'" Our Heavenly Father and Jesus are both at work, and we should be as well. God is not asking us to do anything that He Himself is not doing. If you read the book of Proverbs, you will find numerous verses of scripture condemning the slothful and the sluggard. The Bible is very clear about being a good steward with the responsibilities God gives us, including our work. I believe His Word shows there is dignity in work.

Taking into consideration what is stated above, you need to maintain balance in your life. Yes, a good work ethic is important, but it needs to be balanced with the other responsibilities you have in life, such as family, your spiritual life, recreation, and your physical well-being. A good work ethic is what you do while you are at work and being the best worker you can be while you are there. It means taking personal responsibility for your own conduct and being respectful of your employer and other staff members. These things can be done and still maintain balance in the other areas of your life.

When I was a teenager, one of my first jobs was working at a gas station. I had various duties, but one of them was to balance and rotate tires on cars. Later on, I had a job working in the tire department of a major department store, and I was again rotating and balancing tires. I learned that the benefit of this would extend the life of the tires, and the ride would be smoother.

Our life is similar to this vehicle maintenance practice in that we need balance in all areas of our lives. Why? So our life will be smoother and perhaps even extend our time here on earth.

Proverbs 25:16 (NIV) reads, "If you find honey, eat just enough, too much of it, and you will vomit."

Honey is good for you. It has some health benefits. But if you eat too much of it, as the scripture says, you will vomit. Too much of a good thing is actually bad for you. There are consequences for your action. I believe the lesson from this verse is that we need to live a balanced life, in moderation if you will.

So what does living a balanced life mean and why is it important? Let us look at four areas of your life and look at them if taken to an extreme—work, recreation, education, and religion.

We all know of people who are obsessed with work. They go to work early and leave late. Their family is neglected. Even when they are with their family, their thoughts are on work. Vacations and days off are never on their radar. Then, we have just the opposite. People who never work and often depend on others for their livelihood. They are perfectly content to let others provide for them. Both of these are not how life is meant to be. Work is ordained in the Bible. Scripture also says that God works. Work is honorable and necessary. But even God says to take a day off, just as He did when He created heaven and the earth. It recharges us. Jesus also spent time in the garden, on the lake, and at the mountains. We should all learn from their lessons.

The same principle applies in the area of recreation. Everyone needs that certain something in their life that helps them relax and get away from the problems of everyday life. But we need to be cautious that it does not dominate our life. *You are a servant to anything that controls you. It is your master. What we need is to make things our servant and not let it become our master.*

There is a news correspondent that often appears on television. He also writes an editorial that appears weekly in many major newspapers across the nation. I have tried to read his editorials, but he uses words that I do not understand. They are not words used in everyday conversation, so I have quit reading his columns. Maybe the problem is that I am not well educated. Or it could be that he applies his education in a way that is not beneficial to the general population. I have also seen people that continually go to college, but they never apply what they have learned. *Knowledge, without application, is no better than not having knowledge.*

On the other hand, there are people that are uneducated. Many times, to the point that they are dependent upon society for their support, and they never contribute anything for the betterment of others.

Please do not misunderstand what I am stating here. I am a firm believer in education and the pursuit of wisdom. I believe it is what makes one person more successful than another. Again, *Proverbs 24:5* reads, "A wise man has great power, and a man of knowledge increases strength." There is power and strength in being educated. What I am saying is that a proper balance is nedded in the lives of both of these types of individuals.

The same thing applies to religion. There are some people who flaunt their religion so much that others will avoid them. They are just not enjoyable to be around, and it will even hurt their Christian witness. On the other hand, there are those that religion means nothing to them. These are also people we will avoid. Let me state—there is a great difference in being religious and being spiritual. The Pharisees and Sadducees were religious, but Jesus condemned them because their hearts were not right with God. We need godly wisdom and understanding to know how to properly apply and share our faith with others. Balance is the key.

Look in your Bible at *Matthew 6:25–34*. Here Jesus tells us not to worry about what we should eat, drink, or what we should wear because God will provide those things for us. Some people read those verses and believe they can just sit back and God is going to place those things in their lap. They think that they have no need to work or be a good steward of what God has given them. Throughout the book of Proverbs, Solomon condemned the sluggard. Also, in *2 Thessalonians 3:10 (KJV)*, Paul instructs us, "For even, when we were with you, this we commanded you, that if any would not work, neither should he eat." *A thought question would be, "What brings more glory to God, someone that never works or contributes to society, saying God will provide, or the person that takes the gifts, abilities, and opportunities God has given him or her, and faithfully utilizes them to the benefit of themselves and others?"*

There are so many areas of life that can get out of balance. Accordingly, each of us has a different area of weakness in which we can have excess, and the end result can be harmful. As too much honey is not good for you, we must strive to keep balance in our life as we place our focus on making God our master and serve none other than Him.

In conclusion, I would like to look at one more passage of scripture from Proverbs. As you read this, replace work of the sluggard for field of the sluggard and see how it might apply to an individual's work ethic. *Proverbs 24:30–34 (NIV)* says:

> I went past the field [work] of the sluggard,
> past the vineyard of the man who lacks judgment;
> thorns had come up everywhere, the ground was

covered with weeds, and the stone wall was in ruins. I applied my heart to what observed and learned a lesson from what I saw; A little sleep, a little slumber, a little folding of the hands to rest—and poverty will come on you like a bandit and scarcity like an armed man [or like a beggar].

Again, I believe that we all work for ourselves, regardless of who signs our paycheck, and that ultimately, we will be rewarded for our efforts. *The bottom line is all that we do is to bring glory to God.*

Dealing with Adversity

As we continue our study of becoming a servant after God's own heart, let us look at how God uses adversity, trials, and tribulations in our life to strengthen our heart for Him.

You have just accepted Jesus as your Lord and Savior. Now all of your problems will be resolved. No more financial problems for me. I am going to enjoy good health; no issues with my family or marriage. Right! After all, the Bible says in *John 14:13–14 (KJV)*, "And whatever ye shall ask in my name, that will I do, that the Father may be glorified in the Son. If ye shall ask anything in my name, I will do it."

Do these verses not state that if we pray about something, in the name of Jesus, our prayer will be answered? If this is true, then why are people not healed of disease when we ask God to heal them? Why do we still have financial problems, family problems, unresolved issues in relationships, problems at work, health problems, and even problems in our religion and faith?

Another thought is *why me, Lord?* Admit it; we have all said it, or at least thought it, probably on numerous occasions. Why me, Lord? Why am I going through this really difficult time in my life? I am a good person. Then we go through the good things or deeds we have done. Or we go through a list of the sins or bad things we have not done. Maybe we compare ourselves to others to justify our actions, that we are a really good person and should not be going through this trial in our life. We may even question God or even become bitter at Him for letting this happen to us. *Is this not true?*

So the question is, "Why did God let this happen to me?" Or maybe a better question is, "Why do bad things happen to good people?" Why are all of the problems we face not resolved when we become a Christian and ask God in prayer to remove them? Why, as a Christian do, we still face adversity?

Look at what the Bible says in *James 1:2–4 (NIV):* "Consider it pure joy, my brothers, whenever you face trials of many kinds, because you know that the testing of your faith develops perseverance. Perseverance must finish its work so that you may be mature and complete, not lacking anything." This says that we face many trials to test our faith. This states that we are to persevere or stand firm in our faith so that we will be mature and complete in our walk with God. *How do we know how strong our faith is if it is never tested?*

Why did God create mankind?

To help understand adversity and attempt to explain its purpose in our lives, I submit to you that it is my belief that God created us to love and fellowship with Him. If God gave us a life without trials and tribulations when we became a Christian, how many people would profess to be a Christian because they would receive a trouble-free life instead of loving our Heavenly Father? *That would be a false faith* based on what we receive from God but not out of our love of God. If, in fact, we lived a trouble-free life after becoming a Christian, would it matter who we married? After all, we would have a good marriage. Would it matter what job or occupation we had since we would have no financial problems? We could eat anything we wanted and neglect a healthy lifestyle because we would have no bad health issues. And it would not matter who our friends were or the friends of our children because we would have a life without problems. Who then would actually be in control of your life—you or God? *God in His wisdom knew that His children had to face the same problems in life as nonbelievers so they would truly love Him and place their faith in Jesus as Lord and Savior*

Look at what *Psalm 23:4 (KJV)* tells us about adversity: "Yea, though I walk through the valley of the shadow of death, I will fear no evil; for thou art with me; thy rod and thy staff they comfort me."

Notice that we must go through the valley of the shadow of death, not around it. We must go through our adversities, trials, tribulations, and problems. But also, note from the scripture that "thy rod and thy staff they comfort me."

Since most of us, in current times, do not use a rod or staff, what would this refer to in our life today? To answer this question, *John 14:15–18 (KJV)* states:

> If you love me, keep my commandments. And I will pray the Father, and he shall give you another Comforter, that he may abide with you forever; Even the Spirit of truth, whom the world cannot receive, because it seeth him not, neither knoweth him; but ye know him; for he dwelleth with you, and shall be in you. I will not leave you comfortless; I will come to you.

Why would God need to send the comforter, being the Holy Spirit, if we did not face adversity? Why would we need comfort if all of our problems were resolved when we placed our faith in Jesus as our Lord and Savior?

Where else do we receive comfort today? I believe we get comfort from reading and studying the Bible. Look at *Romans 15:4 (KJV)*: "For whatever things were written aforetime (in earlier times) were written for our learning, that we, through patience and comfort of the scriptures, might have hope."

We could conclude that the Holy Spirit and the Holy Bible give us comfort and hope today. They are our rod and our staff as we deal with adversity in our lives.

Think about some of the people in the Bible that faced adversity—David, Joseph, Job, and Paul, just to name a few.

If you study the life of King David, you will find he repeatedly faced one battle after another. *Is that not the way of our life?* It seems we get past one trial or tribulation and then something else happens. Life is one battle after another—and it will be that way all of our life.

Joseph was sold into slavery by his brothers. He was falsely accused of misconduct with Potiphar's wife and was thrown into prison.

The story of Job is well known and documented. But look at how Job responded to his wife and three friends when they accused him of some sin that caused his adversity. From *Job 27:3–6 (KJV):*

> All the while my breath is in me, and the
> spirit of God is in my nostrils; My lips shall not
> speak wickedness, nor my tongue utter deceit.
> God forbid that I should justify you; till I die
> I will not remove mine integrity from me. My
> righteousness I hold fast, and will not let it go;
> my heart shall not reproach me as long as I live.

Can you feel Job's intensity and how he clung to his integrity? He would not let anything pry it away from him—even when facing great adversity.

You never know the true character or heart of a person until they face adversity. This is when their true character and integrity are revealed. *Anyone can have good character and integrity if they are never tested.*

Another biblical example of adversity is Saul (later to become Paul). I encourage you to read about Paul's conversion experience on the road to Damascus from *Acts 9:1–17*. Look especially at verse 16 where Jesus tells Ananias about Saul: "For I will show him how great things he must suffer for my name's sake." Then read in *2 Corinthians 11:22–30*, where Paul tells of all the hardships he faced while proclaiming that Jesus is Lord and Savior. You can also find additional scripture that support Paul's adversity in *Acts 20:22–24*. As you study these passages from the Bible about Paul, consider this—*what changed Saul, the persecutor of the early church and followers of Jesus, to Paul, the great missionary? The man that was told beforehand all the hardships he would face for proclaiming the gospel of Christ?* The answer is that Paul met the risen Savior, Jesus Christ, and it changed his life forever. He was convinced Jesus was the Messiah, the only begotten Son of God.

Take note that none of the biblical characters I referenced escaped adversity. *Notice also that God blessed their lives and used each of them to serve Him in a great and mighty way.* So He will also bless us if we are faithful to His calling.

If our lives were free from persecution and trial, if we had everything we wanted and had no problems, what would we truly know about our Heavenly Father? Would we realize our need of Him and for Him and how He is continually working in our lives? Would we see and experience His awesome power and grace?

If we compare adversity to an athlete, what makes the athlete stronger and better—ease or hard work? What makes a muscle stronger—resistance or idleness? Facing the trials and tribulations of life is what makes us stronger, and it makes us realize we cannot handle life's problems on our own. We need God in a great and powerful way, and one way our need of Him is revealed is through adversity.

Philippians 4:6 (NIV) says, "Do not be anxious about anything, *but in everything,* by prayer and petition, with thanksgiving, present your requests to God."

When I face adversity, it is really difficult to be thankful. But according to *Philippians 4:6,* we are to express thanksgiving "in everything." When we are faced with trials and tribulations and we are experiencing difficulties beyond our control, we are to be thankful. *Why would God instruct us to be thankful when we are facing adversity?*

I believe there are several reasons why God, in His infinite wisdom, tells us to be thankful in all things, especially in adversity. First, it gets our minds and attention off our difficult situation. We look for something good in our lives for which we are thankful. God knows we need to think about things other than our problems and to think about the blessings in our life. This helps us get through the valley of adversity.

Second, we are forced to concentrate on the positive instead of the negative. It is much more difficult to have negative thoughts when our heart is grateful and we are praising God. One of the ways I am able to lift my spirit when I am depressed is to think about the positive things from my past. I review how God blessed me beyond what I ever envisioned or imagined.

Another reason we are to be thankful is that we see God at work in our lives. Too often, when things are going badly, we have a tendency to blame God for our problems. Being thankful shows us that God is indeed in control. *Is God's power revealed more during good times or bad? Do we see God's hand at work in our strength or our weakness?*

What are some reasons why God allows adversity in our lives? What lessons is He trying to teach us?

- Sometimes God wants to get our attention. Maybe it is to bring us back from a broken fellowship with Him or to cleanse us from some sin or iniquity in our life.
- To remind us of His love for us. *Hebrews 12:5–6 (KJV)* says, "And ye have forgotten the exhortation which speaketh unto you as unto children. My son, despise not thou the chastening of the Lord, nor faint when thou art rebuked of him; For who the Lord loveth he chasteneth, and scourgeth every son who he receiveth."
- For self-examination. Am I doing God's will? Are there areas of my life which I need to change?
- To teach us to hate evil as God does.
- To cause us to reevaluate our priorities.
- To test our works or our faith as we saw earlier in *James 1:2–4.*
- To let others see how we react to adverse situations. This is a part of our Christian witness.
- God may give us adversity to use as a testimony for others and use us to benefit others who may experience similar circumstances. This would be a part of our Christian testimony.
- There are times when adversity is the consequence of our sin or another person's sin.
- God may be using the adversity to prepare you for some special ministry.

As we consider the reasons God takes us through the tough times of life, let's look at *Romans 8:28 (NIV)* and see what God can do in us and through us: "And we know that in all things God works for the good of those who love him, and have been called according to his purpose." Sometimes, we have to look for the good, but when God is working in us, He can and will eventually bring good from our adversity. It just may take time, but we will see His hand at work in our lives if we submit to Him and let His power work in us. Maybe God is working to strengthen you to grow more of a servant's heart.

To repeat something I stated earlier, *how do you know you have faith if it is never tested? How do you know how strong your faith is if you never face adversity?*

When do we see God move the greatest in our lives—in our strengths or in our weaknesses? Second Corinthians 12:9–10 (KJV) tells us:

> And he said unto me, My grace is sufficient for thee; for my strength is made perfect in weakness. Most gladly, therefore, will I rather glory in my infirmities, that the power of Christ may rest upon me. Therefore, I take pleasure in infirmities, in reproaches, in necessities, in persecutions, in distresses for Christ's sake; for when I am weak, then I am strong.

In our own strength, we tend to forget about God. We think we can handle life's situations on our own. But in our weaknesses, we truly see His hand at work in our lives. When we are weak, we realize how much we need and depend on God.

I believe God wants good things for us, and sometimes He must let us face adversity to truly reveal Himself to us. Ultimately, God is doing things in our best interest, and He wants us to live life more abundantly. *Isaiah 40:29–31 (KJV) tells us:*

> He giveth *power* to the faint; and to those who have no might he *increaseth strength*. Even the youths shall faint and be weary, and the young men shall utterly fall. But they that wait upon the Lord shall *renew their strength;* they shall mount

up with wings like eagles; they shall run, and not
be weary; and they shall walk, and not faint.

Where does our strength come from to endure adversity? Our
strength to endure and persevere through trials and adversity comes
from God—not us individually—and He is glorified and honored
through our faithfulness. I really like this statement: "Faith in God
includes faith in His timing." We have to go through the adversity in
God's timing, not ours.

What do you see?

*Have you ever read a verse of scripture many times and one day
a new meaning just jumps out at you?* God's Word is so very special.
You can read it over and over again and still gain new insight and
meaning. God is able to use it specifically for each of us at this particular time or season in our life. He will also reveal certain thoughts
to one of His children for them to share with others. I believe this
is what *Hebrews 4:12 (NIV)* is saying: "For the word of God is living and active. Sharper than any double-edged sword, it penetrates
even to the dividing soul and spirit, joints and marrow; it judges the
thoughts and attitudes of the heart." God's Word is just alive and
active today as it was the day it was written.

One morning, I was asked if I knew a passage of scripture that
would uplift a friend who was dealing with some adversity. I was led
to *Psalm 121:1–2 (NIV)*: "I lift up my eyes to the hills—where does
my help come from? My help comes from the LORD, the Maker of
heaven and earth." Some versions of the Bible say mountains instead
of hills.

This is a passage of scripture I have read over many, many times,
but that day, two new thoughts came to me. When I read the Bible, I
like to ask why God chose to put this in the Bible. What is He wanting us to learn and apply in our lives? I also had a friend state that we
should look for God when we are reading Scripture.

As I read this passage, the first thing I saw was "I lift up my
eyes to the hills." *What is God telling us?* I thought about my friend

facing a trying time in life and this thought came to me. *What do the hills or mountains represent?* It could be that the mountains we see are adversity, trials, or tribulation. When that is the situation and we all face adversity throughout our lives, God is saying your help comes from the Maker of heaven and earth. God is our source of strength.

The second thought I had was God is telling us to look at Him and see His glory and His creation. I love to go to the mountains and see the beauty of God's creation. Maybe God is revealing Himself to us by saying look at all I have created—the heaven and earth and all that is within them. Maybe God is saying if I can create all of this, I can take care of your every need. Just look for God and His power in your adversity. God is telling us He is there to carry us through the storm we are currently experiencing. Times like this is when we realize we cannot handle it on our own. This is when God's power is revealed. *Second Corinthians 12:9 (NIV)* reads, "But he (Jesus) said to me, "My grace is sufficient for you, for my power is made perfect in weakness." God reveals His power in our weaknesses. In this way, God receives the glory.

Jesus tells us in *John 14:15–18 (KJV):*

> If you love, me keep my commandments. And I will pray the Father, and He shall give you another Comforter, that he may abide with you forever; Even the Spirit of Truth, whom the world cannot receive, because it seeth him not, neither knoweth him; but ye knoweth him; for he dwelleth with you, and shall be in you. I will not leave you comfortless; I will come to you.

God has sent His Holy Spirit to live within us and give us comfort.

So lift up your eyes. What do you see? Do you see God and His awesome, creative power? Or do you see a mountain of adversity? Let your help come from God, the Maker of heaven and earth. Let God mold your heart through the trials, tribulation, and adversity as you are becoming a servant after God's own heart.

Yes, God is faithful, and He can move mountains if He chooses to do so. Maybe the mountain that God moves is the mountain of adversity that we face. And He could answer each of our prayers exactly the way we pray them—in the name of Jesus. But His ways are not our ways and His wisdom greatly exceeds our thoughts. In God's wisdom, He always does what will bring glory and honor to His holy and righteous name. We are to be faithful and trust in His wisdom, especially when we are facing adversity.

The bottom line in why we continually face adversity is it reveals our great need of God. We encounter things we cannot handle or take care of with our own strength, and without Him, it lets us see and feel His awesome power at work in our life and in the lives of others. It brings glory and praise to God.

Becoming a Faithful Servant

First Timothy 6:7 (KJV) says, "For we brought nothing into this world, and it is certain we can carry nothing out."

I want to show you, in my opinion, how YOU CAN TAKE IT WITH YOU!

No, that statement is not an error. I must admit that as a former banker, that whenever there was a death of a customer, their money was still in their account after the funeral. I have never seen a withdrawal from a checking account for the purpose of "use in the hereafter." Their house was still here as well as any farmland or other real estate they may have owned. They did not physically carry with them any of their earthly possessions. I think the key word in the verse is "carry."

But I want to show you how, I think, you can take it with you. "And he said unto them, Take heed, and beware of covetousness; for a man's life consisteth not in the abundance of the things which he possesseth" *(Luke 12:15 KJV).*

What does it mean to covet? To covet means to long to possess something that belongs to another, to desire unreasonably or unlawfully, or to be excessively eager for gain. The scripture basically says, "Do not be greedy. Do not desire worldly things. Real life is not in our possessions." We are to guard our hearts against coveting. To guard is to protect, and in this case, guard our hearts against coveting.

So how then are we going to take it with us?

Matthew 6:19–21 (KJV) says:

> Lay not up for yourselves treasures upon earth, where moth and rust doth corrupt, and where thieves break through and steal, But lay up for yourselves treasures in heaven, where neither moth nor rust doth corrupt, and where thieves do not break through nor steal; For where your treasure is, there will your heart be also.

So what are some things that the world calls treasures? Stocks and bonds, certificates of deposits, cash, retirement accounts, real estate, gold and silver, jewels, and other precious metals.

What are intangible assets we may possess? Time, talents, gifts, abilities, and opportunities.

I want you to notice something about all of these tangible "treasures"—they all can be either lost, stolen, or depreciate in value (would this not be where moth and rust corrupt?) *Proverbs 23:4–5 (NIV)* reads, "Do not wear yourself out to get rich; have the wisdom to show restraint. Cast but a glance at riches, and they are gone, for they will surely sprout wings and fly off to the sky like an eagle." *Has this ever happened to worldly treasures?*

From the passage of scripture above, what are we told about "treasures in heaven"? First, we are not told what those treasures will be. But just remember, we do not know the mind of God and how creative He is in His thinking. I do not know this, but I believe they are greater than we can imagine.

Second, they will not be stolen, lost, or depreciate in value. *Does this not imply that our heavenly treasures are permanent from what we are told that in Matthew 6:20?*

Third, *when God asks us to do something and we step out in obedience, in faith, does God not always bless us greater than what we envision or imagine? Why would He not do it in this situation?*

Something else about our treasures; what you treasure may be different than what I treasure. Your gifts and abilities are different from mine. But we are instructed by God to use our "earthly treasures" to build our "treasures in heaven."

So the question is, "Where is your heart?" Is it on worldly things or on heavenly things? I believe these verses state that if your heart is right, you can take it with you by "building your treasures in heaven." *Think about this; if you use your worldly assets to build treasures in heaven, is that not taking it with you?* I must admit, I do not know what the treasures in heaven are or will be, but I want them. Only God knows what treasures we are building in heaven, but His treasures are beyond what we can grasp in our humanly thinking.

In this situation, are we not exchanging one asset for another? Just like if you take cash and purchase real estate, you just exchanged one asset for another. If you then sold the real estate and put the sales proceeds into a certificate of deposit, again, you just exchanged one asset for another.

Here we take an earthly asset and invest into our heavenly future, and hopefully these new investments (heavenly treasures) will continue to grow and compound. Remember back in our first session when we discussed spiritual compounding. And maybe, just maybe, these heavenly investments will continue to compound even after you have gone to your eternal reward in heaven.

How else can you build your treasures in heaven if it is not by using your tangible and intangible assets you possess? I cannot think of anything.

The next question is "How do we build our treasures in heaven?" I think the answer comes from 1 Timothy 6:17–20 (NIV):

> Command those who are rich in this present world, not to be arrogant nor to put their hope in wealth, which is so uncertain, but to put their hope in God, who richly provides us with everything for our enjoyment. Command them to do good, to be rich in good deeds, and to be generous and willing to share. In this way they will lay up treasure for themselves as a firm foun-

dation for the coming age, so that they may take
hold of the life that is truly life.

Let us look together at an interesting breakdown of these verses.

It starts in verse 17 with "command," while the KJV says "charge." This means to instruct or exhort with authority, to impose a task of responsibility, or to give an authoritative order.

Who, then, is this command or instruction given? It is given to those who are rich in this present world.

What are they instructed not to do? They are not to be arrogant or to be full of pride, and they are not to put their hope in their wealth.

Why are they given this command? They were given this command because wealth and riches are uncertain; they sprout wings and fly away, as stated in Proverbs 23:4–5. Our earthly wealth is not permanent.

Where are they to put their hope since wealth is uncertain? They are to put their hope in God, the living God. *Why?* Because He richly provides us with everything for our enjoyment.

In verse 18, what are they commanded or instructed to do (again, they are commanded)? They are commanded to do good, to be rich in good deeds, and to be generous and willing to share. *There is a key word in verse 18, willing. Second Corinthians 9:7 (NIV) tells us,* "Each man should give what he has decided in his heart to give, not reluctantly or under compulsion, for God loves a cheerful giver." God loves a willing giver. Notice the verse says *and*, not *or*; we are commanded to do all these things listed in the verse.

From verse 19, *from where does the treasure for a firm foundation come?* The treasure comes from doing those things listed in verse 18—doing good, rich in good deeds, generous, and willing to share.

And what is the reason for laying up treasures for this firm foundation? The reason is so they may take hold of the life that is truly life. The KJV says that they may lay hold on eternal life. Consider again how long eternity will last. It has no end.

Going back to verse 17, where it states God richly provides us with everything for our enjoyment, think about this—what gives you the most pleasure in life? Is it not when you do something good or beneficial for another individual? Does that not make you feel really good? Look at what *Proverbs 11:24–25 (NIV)* says: "One man gives freely, yet gains even more; another withholds unduly, but comes to poverty. A generous man will prosper; he who refreshes others will himself be refreshed." Only God could come up with a plan where the more you give, the more you are blessed. This is an amazing life application principle—compounding our generosity and good deeds.

Look again at verse 18 from *1 Timothy 6:* (1) That they do good, (2) that they be rich in good works, (3) ready to distribute, and (4) willing to communicate. If we do these things, what are we promised? We are promised that we may lay a firm foundation for our life in heaven. That we are laying up in store for ourselves a good foundation against the time to come, and we are building our "treasures in heaven."

Now look at a challenge from verse 20: "Keep that which is committed to thy trust." What is a trustee? A trustee is a person who holds and manages property or possessions for another person. In this case, of what are we a trustee? We are trustees of those things God has given to us. We can take it with us by doing those things with our money, talents, abilities, time, and opportunities, which will help others and will help build God's kingdom. We are to do things that will have a lasting benefit on the lives of people, even for generations to come after we have gone to be with the Lord, and that will build treasures in heaven that will last for eternity.

Consider this concerning building your treasures in heaven. If your actions on this earth are for the Lord and your investments are for your future in heaven, your actions now will continue in the lives of others after you have gone to be with the Lord. Will those investments not continue to build your treasures in heaven, even though you are no longer here on earth? You are, in effect, investing the principle in heaven, and the investment or heavenly treasures will continue to compound throughout eternity. To me, this is how we become a servant after God's own heart.

How then can we build or obtain these treasures?

There are so many unique ways we can build our treasures in heaven that it would be virtually impossible to start listing them.

They are unique in that each of us will have individual areas in which we can contribute that are in accordance with our own personal beliefs, interests, skills, and talent. But we can go back to the general items God listed in 1 Timothy 6 to get some ideas:

- Lead someone to Jesus, who, in turn, might lead another to Jesus. Share your faith and testimony.
- Teach godly principles to your children and grandchildren. Then they will teach godly principles to their children and grandchildren. Willing to communicate and that they do good.
- There are numerous ministries of service that we can support with our money, time, and talents.
- Use your money to help others in need or to further God's kingdom and His ministries. Ready to distribute, generous, and rich in good works. This category is unlimited to the potential.

Something really amazing is that God may be preparing you for a special ministry—one that is unique, just for you. He may place people, events, trials, situations, opportunities, and even where you live or have lived in preparation for this special ministry.

A biblical example of this would be Moses. From the second chapter of Exodus, look at how God spent many years of Moses's life preparing him to lead the Israelites to the promised land.

This preparation of Moses started when he was an infant. He was raised in Pharoah's house by Pharoah's daughter. This gave him access to Pharoah. This also gave him knowledge in how to deal with Pharoah and the Egyptians and the culture of Egypt.

Moses probably would have never fled to Midian if he had not killed the Egyptian. God used this event in Moses's life for him to go to Midian. Then he spent many years in the desert of Midian, being prepared on how to live in the desert. This prepared Moses to lead the Israelites through the desert.

Another biblical example would be the apostle Paul, from Acts 22:1–14 and Philippians 3:4–6. We see from both of these passages that Paul was a zealot. He was passionate about what he did. God saw this characteristic in Paul, just as He saw the heart in King David. God used that trait in Paul in a great and mighty way in that time in history, and it is even touching lives today through his writings in the New Testament.

Paul's background prepared him for his ministry.

God may be doing something in your life, just as He did with Moses and Paul, to prepare you for some special, unique ministry. Why could God not do the same thing in you and me?

I really hope you grasp the message about building your heavenly treasures I am trying to convey. Think of it like savings and investing for your retirement. You are taking assets you have today and investing them with the return on your investment for future use. In this case, it will be for that time when you have gone to heaven. *This is truly investing for your future.*

No seed, no harvest

I grew up in a small farming community in West Texas. Many of my friends are farmers. In the springtime, they prepared the soil for planting. When the conditions are right, they plant their crops. *If they left the seed in the barn instead of planting them, what would happen?* Nothing at all would happen. The seed actually, over time, may have rotted or have been eaten by mice. *What is the lesson for us in this?*

But when the seed is planted, properly cared for, and the right weather conditions exist, it will produce more fruit and more seed. The seed's purpose is to produce, but for it to be productive, it must be planted. The important thing is that it grows and reproduces. Another consideration is when the farmer has planted the seed; he does not want the seed back the same as when he planted them. He wants them to grow and hopefully produce a bountiful crop and yield even more seed for future crops.

Your life is like the farmer's seed. You can either plant the seeds or your wealth, gifts, and talents, or you can leave them in the barn. You have the power to decide what you will do. Remember this thought from leadership author and speaker John Maxwell: *"You cannot harvest what you have not planted. You cannot harvest where you have not planted."* I would like to add you cannot harvest if you have not planted. Think about how this applies to your life. Yes, you will reap what you sow. Are you sowing seeds of success, mediocrity, or failure?

> A good man out of the good treasure of the heart bringeth forth good things, and an evil man out of the evil treasure bringeth forth evil things. *(Matthew 12:35 KJV)*

> Now he that planteth and he that watereth are one; and every man shall receive his own reward according to his own labor. *(1 Corinthians 3:8 KJV)*

We are rewarded according to our own labor or effort. We reap what we sow, and we receive the benefit of what we sow, but we will also suffer the consequences. We would be wise to listen to God's warning about sowing and reaping. When God gives us a warning, is it not to protect us and for our benefit?

Second Corinthians 9:6 (NIV) reads, "Remember this; Whoever sows sparingly will also reap sparingly, and whoever sows generously will also reap generously." Then *verse 10 from that same chapter* says, "Now he who supplies seed to the sower and bread for food will also supply and increase your store of seed and will enlarge the harvest of your righteousness." Notice God will supply the increase if we have a faithful, willing heart to plant the seed—to do good, good deeds, generous, and willing to share.

Something else to remember—you do not eat the fruit or harvest the crop the day you plant the seed. In fact, someone other than you may eat the fruit or harvest the crop from the seeds you plant. That is great because it is all a part of God's plan for the growth of His kingdom.

Two biblical examples of this would be Moses and King David. Moses led the Israelites to the promised land, but he was not permitted to take them into the promised land.

David wanted to build the temple for God, and he made much of the preparations for the temple, but Solomon was the one who built the temple.

First Corinthians 3:6–9 (NIV) states:

> I (Paul) planted the seed, Apollos watered it, but God made it grow. So neither he who plants nor he who waters is anything, but only God who makes things grow. The man who plants and the man who waters have one purpose, and each will be rewarded according to his own labor. For we are God's fellow workers; you are God's field, God's building.

Please notice that we are God's fellow workers, God's field, and God's building.

So what seeds are you planting in yourself to become a servant after God's own heart?

What seeds are you planting in your children and grandchildren, so they will become servants after God's own heart?

What are you planting in others, so they will become servants after God's own heart and that they know that is where your heart is also?

Watering and refreshing

Your children are your greatest joy and your biggest heartache. That is a statement I have made numerous times, and I have never had anyone question that it is not true. We try, as parents, to instill values and godly principles in our children. And we get great joy when we see that *they get it.* We rejoice when they are reaping what we have sown in them. We are heartbroken when they face troubles, trials, and other problems. We often feel helpless.

I believe the same is true with God. He has given us principles for us to live by, as written throughout the Bible, and it brings Him joy when He can say, "They got it" when God sees us bearing the fruit of His biblical teaching and instruction.

There is one principle from the Bible that I would like to share my thoughts with you. To me, this is an amazing principle for living an abundant life with others and how to be good members of society. I want to utilize two different versions of the Bible because I believe both have a tremendous way of stating God's instructions to us.

First, from the King James Version, *Proverbs 11:24–25:* "There is he that scattereth, and yet increaseth; and there is he that withholdeth more than is fitting, but it tendeth to poverty. The liberal soul shall be made fat, and he that watereth shall be watered also himself." This reads that we gain by giving away or doing good for others but that we lose by withholding good from others. I think that it is interesting that God used water to illustrate this point. Water is vital and essential for life. We cannot survive without water. In the context of relationships, is God not saying that the good we do for others is essential and vital? Is He not also saying that the more we give, the more we will receive back for our kind deeds? To me, this is an amazing, awesome principle God has given us. We are to build up our fellow man or woman, and in return, we will also be built up and increase. And often, when we do good for others, they are encouraged to also do good for others. It has a compounding or multiplying effect.

Now let us look at this same verse from the New International Version, *Proverbs 11:24–25*: "One man gives freely, yet gains even more; another withholds unduly, but comes to poverty. A generous man will prosper; he who refreshes others will himself be refreshed." Refresh means to give strength or energy to something or someone and to revive or restore to the original or better state.

When we refresh others, we give them new strength or energy to face their problems, and we restore them to their former condition or even better than they were before. But wait—there is more. We, the giver of the good deed, are also refreshed. We are strengthened and energized to a condition even better than we were before. Again, this is an amazing principle from God. This shows God's love for us in that He wants us to build up each other, and in return, He builds us up accordingly. Look at what *1 Thessalonians 5:11 (NIV)* states: "Therefore, encourage one another and build each other up, just as in fact you are doing."

The world needs light

Can you recall the darkest place you have ever been? When our children were young, we took a family trip to Carlsbad Caverns in New Mexico. The tour guide took us to a place deep into the cavern and then turned out the lights. I must admit, it was kind of scary. There have been times since then that I thought how it would be if the lights did not come back on. How would we be able to find the path back to the surface?

With that thought in mind, let's look at *Psalm 119:105 (KJV):* "Thy word is a lamp unto my feet, and a light unto my path." This is one of those verses of scripture that I have read many times and always thought about how God gives us guidance and direction, so we can make wise decisions. I never really concentrated or studied the verse for a deeper message. So many times, I think we read over a scripture or Bible passage, but we do not really focus on what God is saying to us. But I would like to take this verse and expand on it somewhat concerning our study about becoming a servant after God's own heart.

Throughout the Bible, God addresses the contrast of light and dark.

Proverbs 4:18–19 (NIV) says, "The path of the righteous is like the first gleam of dawn, shining ever brighter till full light of day. But the way of the wicked is like deep darkness, they do not know what makes them stumble."

Matthew 5:16 (KJV) reads, "Let your light so shine before men, that they may see your good works, and glorify your Father, who is in heaven." *What does it mean to let your light shine before men?* This is the ultimate purpose in our good deeds—to bring praise and glory to God.

Colossians 3:17 (NIV) tells us, "And whatever you do, whether in word or deed, do it all in the name of the Lord Jesus, giving thanks to God the Father through him."

I love what leadership expert John Maxwell says: "Your candle loses nothing when it lights another." This is true; our candle or light does not dim or lose its glow when it lights another. In fact, there is more light that is given off because there are now two candles glowing and giving off light. And often those candles will light even more candles to give off even more light.

Consider how God tells us how to relate to our fellow man. How many verses of scripture and parables does God give us in the Bible where He tells us to take care of each other? He wants us to build up and not to tear down. This applies to any type of relationship. God wants us to make the lives of others better.

Matthew 5:14–16 (NIV) says:

> You are the light of the world. A town built on a hill cannot be hidden. Neither do people light a lamp and put it under a bowl. Instead, they put it on its stand, and it gives light to everyone in the house. In the same way, let your light shine before men, that they may see your good deeds and praise your Father in heaven.

God also lights our path to receive eternal life with Him in heaven through faith in His only begotten Son, Jesus Christ. Jesus says in *John 14:6 (KJV)*, "I am the way, the truth, and the life; No man cometh unto the Father, but by me." This is further supported in *Romans 10:9 (KJV)*, "That if thou shalt confess with thy mouth the Lord Jesus, and shalt believe in thine heart that God hath raised him from the dead, thou shalt be saved." God's Word lights the path to eternal life in heaven through faith in Jesus.

God gives us another special thought considering *Psalm 119:105* and Jesus as our Redeemer and Savior. Let us look at two parts of the verse and how it relates to Jesus. Consider, if you will, the words "Thy word" and "the light." *John 1:1 (KJV)* reads, "In the beginning was the Word, and the Word was with God, and the Word was God." Further in that chapter in *verse 14*, "And the Word was made flesh, and dwelt among us (and we beheld his glory, the glory as of the only begotten of the Father), full of grace and truth." The Word is Jesus. Then in *John 8:12 (KJV)*, we find, "Then spoke Jesus again unto them, saying, I am the light of the world, he that followeth me shall not walk in darkness, but shall have the light of life." Look closely at how God ties this together with *Psalm 119:105*.

Thy word is Jesus, and He is the light showing us how to live life to the fullest. To me, this is amazing how God weaves His Scripture together, explaining His guidance for our benefit and protection.

Look at how *Psalm 19:7–11 (NIV)* gives further guidance:

> The law of the LORD is perfect, reviving the soul. The statutes of the LORD are trustworthy, making wise the simple. The precepts of the LORD are right, giving joy to the heart. The commands of the LORD are radiant, giving light to the eyes. The fear of the LORD is pure, enduring forever. The ordinances of the LORD are sure and altogether righteous. They are more precious than gold, than much pure gold; they are sweeter than honey, than honey from the comb. By them is your servant warned; in keeping them there is great reward.

God loves us so much that He tells us in His Holy Bible how we can live an abundant life. He is truly giving light to our path and a lamp to our feet. Search the Scriptures for yourself and may you be blessed by them as you are blessing others.

Using our talents

Several years ago, my wife Elaine was having a conversation with a lady that had a friend who felt unworthy to be a success in her business. Elaine phoned me at work to see if I had any thoughts on how her friend should respond to this person. I really love people that are humble. I believe humility is a godly characteristic and is supported throughout Scripture. Think about which type of people you prefer to be around—a humble person or a boastful, arrogant one that can only talk about their success?

To answer the question of whether we are worthy of success and are we worthy of becoming a servant after God's own heart, please consider why God chooses to bless us. First, I believe it is to bring glory and honor to God. He blesses us, and we give Him the praise. We share this praise with others so that God will be magnified. The second reason God chooses to bless us is so we will be able to bless others. Again, think of this as compounding God's kingdom that we studied in our first session. God blesses us, and we in turn bless others. Then they bless others and the blessings just keep growing and building. And the results are God being further glorified and praised as more and more people are blessed.

Why would God give us talents, gifts, abilities, and opportunities if we are not to use them for the good and benefit of others?

Attitude determines what you see

Often, the difference between success and failure in our pursuit in becoming a servant after God's own heart is attitude. What determines that one sibling achieves success and another does not? Are they not raised in the same environment and have the same opportunity for success? Do they not have the same *excuses* for failure? Please note that I said excuses and not reasons. More often than not, the difference comes down to attitude and individual determination. Too often we can find excuses for our actions, but can we really find legitimate reasons? Consider this quote from leadership expert John Maxwell: "Your attitude is either your best friend or your worst enemy, your greatest asset or your greatest liability."

Let me share with you a biblical illustration to explain my thinking because our attitude often determines whether we see things as opportunities or obstacles. From *Numbers chapters 13 and 14*, we read the story about Joshua, Caleb, and the ten other men sent by

Moses to spy out the land of Canaan prior to the Israelites entering the promised land. When the twelve men returned with their report, ten stated that the land did overflow with milk and honey and fruit, but its inhabitants were giants and their cities were fortified. Ten of these men saw too many obstacles to overcome. Joshua and Caleb stated that the land was an exceedingly good land and that it could be taken by the Israelites. All twelve men saw the giants and that the land was flowing with milk and honey and the fruit. The fruit was clusters of grapes so large that a branch with a single cluster had to be carried on a pole between two men.

What was the difference in the ten spies and Joshua and Caleb? It was their attitude. All twelve saw the giants and the grapes. God told all of them that He would be with them, just like He tells us today. Ten saw obstacles and two saw opportunity for victory and to enter the promised land.

Ten said, "We cannot do this."

Joshua and Caleb said, "With God on our side, the victory is ours."

All twelve had the same opportunity for victory and success. Each one of us has the ability to "see the grapes of opportunity instead of the giants of failure." Does our attitude not determine whether we "enter the promised land" of our lives?

Another biblical example would be the prophet Daniel. Daniel had been taken captive in Babylon. He was a young man in captivity in a foreign country. You would think he would be bitter and angry and that he would work against his captors and try to undermine them. Or you might think he would do whatever crossed his mind—morally or not—because, after all, he was in a foreign country, and no one would know of his actions. What difference would it make? He had been dealt a bad hand and was in an immoral environment. Who would be affected but him if he did not do the right thing? After all, it was his life, and Daniel had *excuses* not to try and give his best. This is where Daniel's attitude determines the direction of his life. From *Daniel 1:8 (NIV)* the Bible states, "But Daniel resolved not to defile himself with the royal food and wine, and he asked the chief official for permission not to defile himself this way." The key word here is *resolved*. To be resolved means to have a firm determination to make the most of our life. It means that Daniel determined, in advance and at a young age, the course for his life.

Is this not the same for all of us? Yes, we can find *excuses* not to try and succeed. Or we can be resolved, just like Daniel, to give our best and contribute to the success of ourselves and others. Each of us individually can take advantage of the opportunities this great nation presents to anyone willing to work and sacrifice. We can determine that we will be givers and not takers as we are becoming a servant after God's own heart. Consider how many other people's lives may be negatively affected when you do not give your best effort!

When we start to go to school, is it not the objective to advance and progress each year and to increase our learning? Do athletic teams not practice to improve instead of staying the same throughout the season? We should be striving to grow and advance, not to stay where we start. We should have the attitude and determination to build up and not tear down and resolve that we will make a godly, spiritual difference in the lives of others.

Consider the story of David and Goliath taken from the seventeenth chapter of 1 Samuel. A review of the scriptures says that the giant Goliath challenged the armies of Israel to send someone to fight with him. The soldiers of Israel all heard Goliath defy them, including the king of Israel, Saul. Yet David, who was a youth and not a soldier, accepted Goliath's challenge. In *1 Samuel 17:45 (KJV)*, David said, "I come to thee in the name of the LORD of Hosts, the God of the armies of Israel, who thou has defied." *Was God not the Lord of all the armies of Israel? What made David stand up to Goliath when the soldiers of Israel would not?* It was his attitude and his belief that God would stand with him. *Verse 47* states, "For the battle is the LORD's, and he will give you into our hands." That is the way it is with you and me. The battles in our lives are the Lord's. We only need to place the battle into His hands and let Him give us the victory over the giants we face. But it is our attitude that determines the effort we will make to achieve the victory.

I wonder how different David's life would have been if he had not accepted the challenge from Goliath. *Would he ever have become the King of Israel? Would God have later stated that he was a man after God's own heart?* The point I want to make is that we determine our future by the decisions we make today. Will we fight, or will we run from the battle? Each time we are faced with a challenge, our faith is tested. *Will we trust God to give us the victory, or will we just accept the consequences of our inaction?* When we engage in the battle, we become stronger, and we start to see God at work in our lives. David was able to use his encounters with the lion and the bear to prepare him for the battle with Goliath. And God will use our experiences to prepare us for future battles. Stand firm and fight the fight before you. God is with you, just as He was with David.

God has equipped each of us with unique gifts, talents, skills, abilities, and opportunities that we can utilize to build up one another. The ways in which we all can do this are unlimited. This shows God can and will use each of us, regardless of our condition and/or season in life.

Hebrews 13:16 (NIV) says, "And do not forget to do good and to share with others, for with such sacrifices God is pleased." We bring joy to God and please Him when we water, refresh, and share our light with others. God has a purpose in everything. Yes, we are to do good deeds to build up each other, but ultimately, we are to do good in the name of the risen Savior, Jesus Christ, and to lead others to accept Him as Lord and Savior. We do this because we love Him and care about others. We do it because we are becoming a servant after God's own heart.

Becoming a Servant After God's Own Heart

During the early 1970s, there was a song titled "Signs" by the Five Man Electrical Band. The chorus of the song was

> Signs. Signs.
> Everywhere there's signs.
> Blocking out the scenery.
> Breaking my mind.
> Do this! Don't do that!
> Can't you read the signs?

There are signs everywhere, warning us of danger if we don't obey the sign. There are warning labels on the food we purchase, on our medicine. And there are highway signs—stop signs, dangerous curves ahead, yield, etc. There are even grooves carved into the side of the highway to warn us if we are veering off the road. The yellow lines by the center strip to warn us of potential danger if we pass the car in front of us.

What would happen if we ignored these signs? We would be exposed to danger if we disobeyed the warning signs. All of these are there for our safety and protection.

Throughout the Bible, God has given us warning signs. If we study the twenty-eighth chapter of the book of Deuteronomy, we find God telling us of the blessings He will bestow upon *us IF we* are obedient to His commands. I know this was written for the children of Israel, but I believe it still applies to us today in America. The first fourteen verses list the blessings: some of them are He will bless our crops and livestock, our enemies will flee from us, He will bless everything we put our hand to, we will be a holy people, God will open the storehouse of heaven, we will have rain in season, we will lend to many nations and borrow from none, we will be the head and not the tail, and we will be at the top and never at the bottom. *Are any of these blessings things we would not want?*

The rest of the chapter, verses 15 through 68, list all the curses we will have *if* we are not obedient to God's commands. God will curse our crops and livestock. We will have confusion. He will curse everything we put our hand to. We will have diseases, fever, and inflammation, scorching heat and drought, and blight and mildew. We will be defeated by our enemies, we will suffer from madness, blindness, and confusion of mind, we will sow much, but harvest little, and we will have family issues and prolonged disasters.

It is also interesting to note these curses, when it comes to foreigners, they will reside with you and will rise above you higher and higher, but you will sink lower and lower. They will lend to you, but you will not lend to them; they will be the head, but you will be the tail.

Look at what Deuteronomy 28:43–44 (Living Bible) states:

> Foreigners living among you shall become richer and richer while you become poorer and poorer. They shall lend to you, not you to them! They shall be the head and you shall be the tail! All these curses shall pursue and overtake you until you are destroyed—all because you refuse to listen to the LORD your God.

Are all these curses not things happening in America today? As of this writing, our national debt exceeds thirty-one trillion dollars, and that does not include unfunded obligations such as government pensions, student loan guarantees, FMNA, GNMA, and loan guarantees for other nations. Then add to this the debt of states, cities, counties, and local school districts. All funded through taxes on the same taxpayers.

Consider all the natural disasters we are having—hurricanes, tornados, earthquakes, wildfires, droughts, and floods. I know, we have always had these, but they are becoming more frequent and more severe.

A major political issue is healthcare. Can you name any family that is not affected by cancer or heart disease? COVID-19?Dementia, Alzheimer's, and autism are illnesses that are becoming more prevalent each year. Today, many of the diseases we thought were under control are starting to become an issue.

Foreigners are becoming much more active in our political system. Many are being elected to Congress, state, and local offices. They are purchasing our major companies and our farmland.

Consider how divided our nation is today over racism, politics, religion, environment, migration, abortion, sexual orientation, and other social issues. In the Old Testament, God normally used a foreign nation to defeat Israel when they were disobedient to Him. Today, God is permitting our own citizens to destroy this great nation. Look at all the division, rioting, looting, stealing, and even killing going on today. American against American. We are in a battle—good against evil, light against dark, sweet and against bitter. America is basically in another Civil War.

We cannot blame God for this. We have in fact thrown Him out of our schools, government, courts, and judicial system. *Why would God protect and preserve a country that has rejected Him and His provisions?* God's truths have not changed. We as a nation have changed and rejected Him.

If we return to Deuteronomy 28:1–2 (NIV), God tells us, "If you fully obey your God and carefully follow all his commands I give you today, the Lord your God will set you high above all the nations on earth. All these blessings will come upon you and accompany you if you obey the Lord your God." Notice He says "fully obey" and "all" His commands. This is not just to be on occasion or when we feel like being obedient. It is to be our life all the time. Think about this: *why would God bless us if we are not obedient to Him?* He has warned us, and He is trying to protect us as stated in the Bible. God's commandments are to enhance our lives, not restrict them, and He is telling us how. Galatians 6:7 (NIV) warns us, "Do not be deceived; God cannot be mocked. A man reaps what he sows." *Are we mocking God today? As a nation, are we not now reaping the harvest of what we have sown?* Consider the things that are approved and accepted today that just a few decades ago were considered immoral. Look at the movie and television industry, the music industry, sexual perversion, and abortion. *In my humble opinion, abortion is the greatest abomination in the history of mankind.*

It has been said that you cannot legislate morality. *But why would you legislate immorality?* The thing that made America great is the very thing that will bring our destruction—freedom. If you cannot accept the responsibility that goes with freedom, then you will lose your freedom. Too many people today are not accepting this responsibility and are exploiting and perverting the freedoms we enjoy.

We must, individually and as a nation, turn back to God. Second Chronicles 7:14 (NIV) guides us, "If my people, who are called by my name will humble themselves and pray and seek my face and turn from their wicked ways, then will I hear from heaven and will forgive their sin and heal their land." Notice the progression that must take place. First is humility, prayer, seeking God, repent from evil, then God will hear our prayers, forgive our sin, and heal our nation. We, as a nation and individually, must act first before God will fulfill this promise. *Why would and should God bless a people who do not honor, reverence, and respect Him?*

This gives us the background for the next portion of our study in this session.

Be prepared and stand firm in the battle

How would you describe a society without God? A lot of what we just reviewed, plus murders, stealing, rioting, uncontrolled crime, deception, lies, and political and corporate corruption. It would be a world void of God's blessings and filled with God's curses.

In New Testament times, when the apostle Paul wrote to the church at Ephesus, he issued a battle cry or warning, not only for them, but it has great application to us in this study. Notice how God incorporates all four incredible gifts from God that we studied in Session 4 earlier into this passage—Jesus, the Holy Spirit, the Bible, and prayer. This is found in *Ephesians 6:10–18 (NIV)*:

> Finally, be strong in the Lord and in his mighty power. Put on the full armor of God so that you can take your stand against the devil's schemes. For our struggle is not against flesh and blood, but against the rulers, against the authorities, against the powers of this dark world and against the spiritual forces of evil in the heavenly realms. Therefore, put on the full armor of God, so that when the day of evil comes, you may be able to stand your ground, and after you have done everything, to stand. Stand firm then, with the belt of truth buckled around your waist, with the breastplate of righteousness in place, and with your feet fitted with the readiness that comes from the gospel of peace [Jesus]. In addition to all this, take up the shield of faith, with which you can extinguish all the flaming arrows of the evil one. Take the helmet of salvation and the sword of the Spirit, which is the word of God [The Bible]. And pray in the Spirit [The Holy Spirit] on all occasions with all kinds of prayers and requests [Prayer]. With this in mind, be alert and always keep on praying for all the saints.

From this passage of scripture, God identifies the enemy, tells us how to prepare for the battle, and what weapons we need to take up against the enemy.

How would you describe the battle we are in today?

My friends, we are in an intense, fierce, spiritual battle today. If you are like me, nearly every conversation with family and friends discusses the decline in morals and how our great nation and the rest of the world are becoming more and more evil and corrupt. And it seems to be escalating faster over the last few years and months.

Together, let us dig into the passage of scripture from *Ephesians 6* as we put on the full armor of God. *From where does our strength for the battle come?* In verse 10, we are told to "be strong in the Lord and in his mighty power." God is with us in this battle, and it will be won in and through His strength and mighty power. The battle is in God's hands, but we are His warriors. God has provided everything we need to fight this battle.

Next, *notice that three times God tells us to take a stand*—"take a stand" in verse 10, "stand your ground" in verse 13, and "stand firm" from verse 14. This tells us to be engaged in the battle, but how can you fight the battle if you are not trained to fight (this is covered later in these verses)? Not one time are we told in this passage to retreat or to be disengaged from the fight. Brothers and sisters, now is the time to stand firm. The spiritual welfare of our children, grandchildren, family, friends, and even the survival of the United States as we know it is at stake.

Who is the enemy, and who is the battle against?

God identifies the enemy in verses 11 and 12. We are fighting against the devil and his schemes. But notice we are also fighting against the rulers, authorities, and those in power in this dark and evil world, as well as the spiritual forces of evil. The rulers and authorities are our politicians and those with the power to make laws and regulations which govern us. Look at all the accusations of corruption against our politicians. Consider all the laws passed or proposed that are against God's biblical truth. Laws have been passed that promote evil over good and darkness over light. Look at what is being shown in movies, television, music, and entertainment industries. *Do they not promote and encourage immorality and perversion?* For some reason, these are people of influence. And this is a fierce part of the battle we are fighting.

What armor has God provided for this battle?

Thankfully, God tells us how to prepare to stand firm in this battle in verse 15: "With your feet fitted with the readiness that comes from the gospel of peace." The gospel of peace is about Jesus, the Prince of Peace. The gospel is that only through faith in Jesus as our Lord and Savior can we be redeemed from the penalty of our sins. Faith in Jesus is the beginning and foundation of our preparation for the battle. Through the gospel of Jesus, we gain truth and righteousness, which are a part of the armor of God. Further, God gives us more armor and protection through the shield of faith and the helmet of salvation. This whole armor of God is for our protection in the battle against the dark and evil forces of this world. God has provided the armor, but it is up to each of us to put it on in preparation for the battle.

What weapons are we told to use in this spiritual battle?

The next thing we are told to do is to grab and hold firmly the "sword of the Spirit, which is the word of God." These are actually two very powerful weapons for war that God has provided for us, the Holy Spirit and the Bible. These two weapons always work together. The Holy Spirit comes to live in you only after you have accepted Jesus as Savior. This is God living in us and providing the power and strength of our Lord as stated in verse 10. Also, for the Bible to be a powerful weapon for you, then you must know what it says and the *truth* contained in it. That can only be accomplished by continuing to read and study it and asking the Holy Spirit to guide you in biblical truth.

What role does prayer play in this battle in which we are to be engaged?

Finally, we are told in verse 18 to "pray in the Spirit on all occasions, with all kinds of prayers and requests…be alert and always keep on praying." Pray that God will guide you and protect you in this intense war against the devil, rulers, authorities, and powers of this dark and evil world, and be alert. Be aware of the lies and deception of the evil one and those in power. And keep on praying. Make prayer a priority and a part of your daily life.

So are you going to heed the battle cry and join in the fight? Are you ready to stand firm, and are you prepared for the battle by daily putting on the whole armor of God? Be a mighty warrior, and may God bless and protect you.

Please note, again, that all four of the gifts from God are a part of the full armor of God. Use them wisely.

Romans 8:31 (NIV) says, "If God is for us, who can be against us?" The victory will come from the Lord.

As we conclude this study, *Becoming A Servant After God's Own Heart*, I would like for you to think seriously with me about the meaning of something. This is a term that is very difficult for most, if not all of us humans, to truly grasp. Yes, we may know the definition, but to fully realize what it means is difficult. Follow with me as we pursue this together.

The word I am referencing is *eternity. How would you describe eternity?* The definition of eternity is time that never ends, infinite time, duration without end, and timeless existence.

Our human minds have difficulty grasping anything without beginning or end. Each day has a beginning and end. Every year a beginning and an end. Even our very life starts at birth and ends at death on this earth.

In an effort to understand eternity, I look at it as a perfect circle. There is no beginning and no end to a perfect circle. It just keeps going but does not end. Another way to describe eternity would be if you started walking east and kept walking all the way around the world, you would never reach west. You would always be going east. That is not true if you started walking north. When you reach the North Pole, you would then start going south.

Eternity is time without end. *Why is this not only important but is, in my opinion, vital to each and every person?* The Bible says that we are going to spend eternity, time without end, in either heaven or hell. Please grasp this in view of eternity. *There is no end in eternity.*

How would you describe hell? Hell is described as a place of eternal misery, torture, and torment.

The story of Lazarus and the rich man gives us a glimpse of hell, from Luke 16:19–31 (NIV):

> There was a rich man who was dressed in
> purple and fine linen and lived in luxury every
> day. At his gate was laid a beggar named Lazarus,

covered with sores and longing to eat what fell from the rich man's table. Even the dogs came and licked his sores. The time came when the beggar died and the angels carried him to Abrahams's side. The rich man also died and was buried. In hell, where he was in torment, he looked up and saw Abraham far away, with Lazarus by his side. So he called to him, "Father Abraham, have pity on me and send Lazarus to dip the tip of his finger in water and cool my tongue, because I am in agony in this fire." But Abraham replied, "Son, remember that in your lifetime you received good things, while Lazarus received bad things, but now he is comforted here and you are in agony. And besides all this, between us and you a great chasm has been fixed, so that those who want to go from here to you cannot, nor can anyone cross over from there to us." He answered, "Then I beg you, father, send Lazarus to my father's house, for I have five brothers. Let him warn them, so that they will not also come to this place of torment." Abraham replied, "They have Moses and the Prophets; let them listen to them." "No, Father Abraham," he said, "but if someone from the dead goes to tell them, they will repent." "He said to him, 'If they did not listen to Moses and the Prophets, they will not be convinced even if someone rises from the dead.'"

Do you believe that the Bible is true? Why would God include this story in the Bible if the description of hell from it was not true and accurate? Why would God include this in the Bible if not to warn us and protect us from hell?

Matthew 13:41–42 (NIV) tells us, "The Son of Man will send out his angels, and they will weed out of his kingdom everything that causes sin and all who do evil. They will throw them into the fiery furnace, where there will be weeping and gnashing of teeth."

How would you describe heaven? Jesus told the thief on the cross, "Today you will be with me in paradise" *(Luke 23:43 NIV).* So paradise is one description of what heaven will be like. A definition of paradise is a very beautiful, pleasant, and peaceful place that seems to be perfect. It is a place of extreme beauty, delight, and happiness.

Revelation 21:1–5 (NIV) states:

> Then I saw a new heaven and a new earth, for the first heaven and the first earth had passed away, and there was no longer any sea. I saw the Holy City, the new Jerusalem, coming down out of heaven from God, prepared as a bride beautifully dressed for her husband. And I heard a loud voice from the throne saying, 'Now the dwelling of God is with men, and he will live with them. They will be his people, and God himself will be with them and be their God. He will wipe away every tear from the eyes. There will be no more death or mourning or crying or pain, for the old order of things has passed away.

We probably have a better image from the Bible of what hell will be like than what heaven will be like. Maybe it is because it is difficult to find the words to accurately describe how wonderful heaven actually will be for us.

So this brings us to the question *the decision of spending eternity in either heaven or hell* (and I have never found another option in the Bible as to where we will spend eternity). According to the Bible, there is only one way to heaven and that is through faith in Jesus Christ as Lord and Savior. That decision is made by each person individually. In the case of Jesus, no decision is a decision, and the decision has eternal consequences or rewards. Jesus is the way, the truth, and the life, and no man comes to the Father, except by Jesus, as stated in *John 14:6 (NIV)* and further supported by *Romans 10:9–*

10 (NIV): "That if you confess with your mouth, 'Jesus is Lord,' and believe in your heart that God raised him from the dead, you will be saved. For it is with your heart that you believe and are justified, and it is with your mouth that you confess and are saved."

For those who believe that God is a God of love and that He would not send anyone to hell, God is a God of love, and He has provided the way or path to heaven and that is through Jesus. If anyone goes to hell, it is because they choose that path instead of the way God has stated and provided.

My friends and family, this is serious. Where you spend eternity is at stake. The consequences of hell are indescribably horrific. *Are you willing to take the chance that heaven and hell are not real?* It is my sincere, fervent prayer that you wisely and prayerfully consider what is stated here. The decision is yours, and there are timeless, eternal consequences or rewards for the decision you make.

Closing prayer

A final personal thought about becoming a servant after God's own heart. This is my prayer for each of you that have taken this journey with me, and these are things we discussed in this study.

> I pray that God would give you:
> Wisdom and discernment like Solomon.
> Integrity like Job.
> Resolve or commitment like Daniel.
> Passion or zeal like Paul.
> And a heart like David.

ABOUT THE AUTHOR

Eddie Hedges is a retired banker with over forty-five years of service in the banking industry. He has served as CEO and president of three community banks in Texas, as well as serving on the board of directors of five banks. He has taught financial seminars in churches and at the Christian Women's Job Corp. He is the author of the book *The Heart of Financial Matters, Seeking a Servant's Heart*, which was the text of the seminars he led.

Since his retirement from banking, Eddie has written numerous devotions and articles. He has been active in his church, having served as a teacher and on various committees. He and his wife, Elaine, are members of Southcrest Baptist Church in Lubbock.

The Hedges live in Lubbock, Texas, and they have four children and ten grandchildren.